The Bush Theatre presents the world premiere of

The God Botherers

by Richard Bean

19 November – 20 December 2003

Cast (In order of appearance)

Keith	Roderick Smith
Ibrahima / Harsha	Sunetra Sarker
Laura	Georgia Mackenzie
Monday	David Oyelowo

Director	William Kerley
Designer	Bob Bailey
Lighting Designer	Tanya Burns
Sound Designer	Mike Winship
Deputy Stage Manager	Lorna Seymour

Press Representation	The Sarah Mitchell Partnership
	020 7434 1944

Graphic Design	Emma Cooke
	design@chamberlainmcauley.co.uk

The God Botherers **was commissioned by The Bush Theatre and received its world premiere at The Bush Theatre, London on 21 November 2003**

We gratefully acknowledge the assistance of
Persil
Comfort
Persil Silk & Wool
courtesy of
LEVER FABERGÉ
in providing Wardrobe Care.

Georgia Mackenzie – Laura

Theatre credits include *Stop Kiss* (Soho Theatre) and *Death of Cool* (Hampstead).

Television credits include *Trial and Retribution VII* (La Plante Productions); *20 Things to Do before You're 30* (Tiger Aspect); *TLC* (Pozzitive TV); *Spine Chillers – Intuition* (BBC); *Judas* (Panorama Films); *Hot Money* (Granada); *Border Café* (Hartswood Films / BBC); *Touch of Frost* (Yorkshire Television); *Up, Rising* (Tiger Aspect); *Passion Killers* (Granada) and *Trust* (Red Rooster).

Film credits include *Possession* (USA Films / Warner Brothers); *County Kilburn* (Watermark); *The Criminal* (Criminal Productions) and *Greenwich Mean Time* (Anvil GMT Films Ltd).

David Oyelowo – Monday

Theatre credits include *Henry VI* (parts 1, 2 and 3); *Richard III, Oroonoko, Volpone*, and *Anthony and Cleopatra* (Royal Shakespeare Company); *Suppliants* (The Gate); *Los Escombros* and *Mirad* (RNT Studio); *A Taste of Honey, Coriolanus* and *Bouncers* (Brave New World); and *The Love of The Nightingale* (Yellow Sky).

Television credits include two series of *Spooks* (Kudos / BBC), winner of Best Drama Series at the 2003 BAFTA Television Awards; *Brothers and Sisters* (BBC); *Maisie Raine* (BBC) and *King of Hearts* (Channel 4).

Film credits include *A Sound of Thunder* (Thunder Films); *Tomorrow La Scala* (BBC Films); *Circles* (BBC Films) and *Dog Eat Dog* (Tiger Aspect). David's performance of the title role in *Henry VI* won him the Ian Charleson Award 2001 for best newcomer in a classical play. He was also the winner of the GAB Award for Excellence 2003.

Sunetra Sarker – Ibrahima / Harsha

Theatre credits include *Airport 2000 – A Night of Sketches* (Stratford East at Greenwich); *One Night* (Stratford East / Moti Roti Prods); *Tale of Two Sisters* (West Yorkshire Playhouse); *Mother Goose* (Royal Northern College) and *House of the Sun* (Pinky / Lakishimi Stratford East).

Television credits include *Eyes Down* (BBC); *Emmerdale* (Yorkshire Television); *City Life: Bloody Foreigners* (Granada); *Doctors* (BBC); *Brookside* (Mersey Television); *Streetlife* (BBC); *Happy Birthday Shakespeare* (BBC); *Playing the Field* (Tiger Aspect / BBC); *Miller Shorts* (BBC); *Starting Out* (Alomo); *Cold Feet* (Granada); *London Bridge* (Carlton); *Wing and a Prayer* (Channel 5); *Women Refugees* (Channel 4); *Flight* (BBC Screen Two); *Soul Survivors* (YTV); *Cracker* (Granada); *Bhangra Girls* (BBC Television Scene) and *Bread* (BBC Television).

Radio credits include *If Music be the Food of Love Mine's a Jam Butty, Shakti, I Should be so Lucky* and *Everybody in the House* (Radio 4) and *The Crack* and *The Fairground* (Radio 5).

Roderick Smith – Keith

Recent theatre credits include *Pat and Margaret* (Salisbury Playhouse); Walt Hemmings in *The Glee Club* (The Bush and The Duchess); *Tragedy: a tragedy* (The Gate); *Best Mates* (RNT tour); *The Winter's Tale* (Southwark Playhouse). Other credits include *Enjoy* (Nottingham Playhouse); *The Birthday Party, Tales From Hollywood, Antigone, Neaptide, Garden of England, True Dare Kiss* and *Command or Promise* (all at RNT); *The Wicked Cooks* and *Outskirts* (Birmingham Rep Studio); *The Beaux' Stratagem* and *Rhinoceros* (The Nuffield Southampton); *Artists and Admirers, The Changeling* and *One Fine Day* (Riverside Studios) and *The Fool* (Royal Court).

Recent television credits include *The Story of Tracy Beaker, The Basil Brush Show, Holby City, The Bill, Doctors,* Sgt Keith Lardner in *Dangerfield – six series.* Also includes *Sam Saturday, Full Stretch, Specials, The Firm, Paradise Club, Playing for Real, Boon, Angels, Destiny, Dr Who* and *The Dick Emery Show.*

Film credits include *Sylvia* (Ariel Films); *In Search of Gregory* (Universal). Roderick has also had two short plays produced by the RNT Studio: *Sunday Morning* and *K. Top.*

Richard Bean – Writer

Richard's stage plays include *Toast* (Royal Court / RNT Studio); *Mr England* (RNT Studio / Sheffield Crucible); *The Mentalists* (RNT / Transformation season); *Under the Whaleback* (Royal Court) and *Smack Family Robinson* (Newcastle Live!). He was co-winner (with Gary Owen) of the 2002 George Devine Award for *Under the Whaleback.*

Radio plays include *Of Rats and Men, Robin Hood's Revenge* and *Unsinkable.*

William Kerley – Director

William is a freelance director of theatre and opera. Recent productions include the award-winning first production of *Jump to Cow Heaven* by Gill Adams at the Edinburgh Festival and Riverside Studios, *Oedipus the King* for the National Youth Theatre, the fiftieth anniversary production of *Gloriana* at the 2003 Aldeburgh Festival, *La Finta Semplice* and *Il Re Pastore* for Classical Opera Company at the ROH Linbury Studio, *Dialogues des Carmelites* and *Manon* at the RSAMD and the world premiere of *The Embalmer* by Giorgio Battistelli for Almeida Opera.

Bob Bailey – Designer

Graduated from Central St. Martin's in 1993. Previous productions include: *Edward Gant's Amazing Feats of Loneliness* (Plymouth Drum); *Stitching* (Traverse, Edinburgh, Bush Theatre, London, UK tour and Berlin); *The Lying Kind* (Royal Court Downstairs) all Directed / Written by Anthony Neilson; *The Lieutenant of Inishmore* (UK tour) Directed by Wilson Milam;

Tosca (Nationale Reisopera, Holland) and *La Ronde* (RADA) both Directed by Carlos Wagner; *Grapes of Wrath* (Finborough) and *Angels in America* (Crucible, Sheffield) both Directed by Phil Willmott; *About Face* (Royal Opera House Education) and *The Baker's Wife* (RAM) both Directed by Jo Davies; *Venezia* (Royal National Theatre Studio / Gate, London) and *Seeds Under Stones* (RSC festival) both Directed by Rebecca Gatward; *Hijra* (Plymouth Drum and Bush, London, Directed by Ian Brown).

In 1999 Bob was awarded Time Out Designer of the Year for *The Happiest Day of my Life* (DV8 Dance Company, UK and European tour). Other designs include *Charley's Aunt* (Sheffield Crucible) Directed by Deborah Paige; *Dancing at Lughnasa* (Jermyn Street) Directed by Gillian King; *Horseplay* and *All Nighter* (Both Dancebites for the Royal Ballet) Choreography by Tom Sapsford; *Good Works* and *Rough Music* (Show of Strength, Bristol). Bob was a recipient of an Arts Council Bursary for Stage Design working at the Bristol Old Vic where productions included *Beaux Stratagem* (costumes); *Enemy of the People* (costumes); *Moll Flanders* (set / costume); *Translations* (set / costume) all for Bristol Old Vic, all directed by Ian Hastings.

Tanya Burns – Lighting Designer

Tanya was awarded the prestigious Arts Foundation Fellowship for Lighting Designers in 1996, and has since gained her MSc in Light and Lighting at UCL's Bartlett School of Architecture. In addition to theatre, she is now a lighting consultant on exhibition, architectural and environmental projects. Recent work includes: Samsung. ITC, Geneva; Samsung Centre, Moscow; Ford, Las Vegas; Nasdaq TV Studios, Times Square New York; Coca Cola at Madison Square Gardens, New York; Samsung Pavillion and Exhibition at the Winter Olympics, Salt Lake City (International Gold Award Winner).

Tanya has worked for many years in British Theatre, covering the West End, London and regional repertory theatres, lighting dance and opera as well as theatre. Her most recent work for The Bush was on the *Naked Talent* season in 2002 and on Simon Burt's *Got To Be Happy* earlier this year.

Mike Winship – Sound Designer

Sound designs include: *Americans* (Arcola); *Stealing Sweets and Punching People* (Latchmere); John Bull's *Other Island* (Tricycle); *Rampage* (Royal Court); *The York Realist* (Royal Court / Strand); *The Trestle at Pope Lick Creek*, *The Changeling*, *Solace* (Southwark Playhouse); *Descent* (Birmingham Rep – The Door); *Tape* (New Venture, Brighton); *A Thought in Three Parts* (BAC); *Deep Throat – Live On Stage* (BAC / Assembly Rooms, Edinburgh); *The Art of Success* (Arcola); *Love upon the Throne* (Comedy / Assembly Rooms, Edinburgh); *The Last Sortie* (New End) and *Tamagotchi Heaven* (Pleasance, Edinburgh).

The Bush Theatre

The Bush Theatre opened in April 1972 in the upstairs dining room of The Bush Hotel, Shepherds Bush Green. The room had previously served as Lionel Blair's dance studio. Since then, The Bush has become the country's leading new writing venue with over 350 productions, premiering the finest new writing talent.

'One of the most vibrant theatres in Britain, and a consistent hotbed of new writing talent.'
Midweek Magazine

Playwrights whose works have been performed here at The Bush include: Stephen Poliakoff, Robert Holman, Tina Brown, Snoo Wilson, John Byrne, Ron Hutchinson, Terry Johnson, Beth Henley, Kevin Elyot, Doug Lucie, Dusty Hughes, Sharman Macdonald, Billy Roche, Tony Kushner, Catherine Johnson, Philip Ridley, Richard Cameron, Jonathan Harvey, Richard Zajdlic, Naomi Wallace, David Eldridge, Conor McPherson, Joe Penhall, Helen Blakeman, Lucy Gannon, Mark O'Rowe and Charlotte Jones.

The theatre has also attracted major acting and directing talents including Bob Hoskins, Alan Rickman, Antony Sher, Stephen Rea, Frances Barber, Lindsay Duncan, Brian Cox, Kate Beckinsale, Patricia Hodge, Simon Callow, Alison Steadman, Jim Broadbent, Tim Roth, Jane Horrocks, Gwen Taylor, Mike Leigh, Mike Figgis, Mike Newell and Richard Wilson.

Victoria Wood and Julie Walters first worked together at The Bush, and Victoria wrote her first sketch on an old typewriter she found backstage.

In over 30 years, The Bush has won over one hundred awards and recently received The Peggy Ramsay Foundation Project Award 2002. Bush plays, including most recently *The Glee Club,* have transferred to the West End. Off-Broadway transfers include *Howie the Rookie* and *Resident Alien.* Film adaptations include *Beautiful Thing* and *Disco* Pigs. Bush productions have toured throughout Britain, Europe and North America, most recently *Stitching. Adrenalin…Heart* will tour to the Tokyo International Arts Festival in March 2004.

Every year we receive over fifteen hundred scripts through the post, and we read them all. According to The Sunday Times:

'What happens at The Bush today is at the very heart of tomorrow's theatre'

That's why we read all the scripts we receive and will continue to do so.

Mike Bradwell   Fiona Clark
Artistic Director   Executive Producer

Support The Bush – Patron Scheme
Be There At The Beginning

The Bush Theatre is a writer's theatre – dedicated to commissioning, developing and producing exclusively new plays. Up to seven writers each year are commissioned and we offer a bespoke programme of workshops and one-to-one dramaturgy to develop their plays. Our international reputation of over thirty years is built on consistently producing the very best work to the very highest standard.

With your help this work can continue to flourish.

The Bush Theatre's Patron Scheme delivers an exciting range of opportunities for individual and corporate giving, offering a closer relationship with the theatre and a wide range of benefits from ticket offers to special events. Above all, it is an ideal way to acknowledge your support for one of the world's greatest new writing theatres.

To join, please pick up an information pack from the foyer, call Nicky Jones, Development Manager on 020 7602 3703 or email development@bushtheatre.co.uk

We would like to thank our current members and invite you to join them!

Rookies
Anonymous
Anonymous
Brian Cox
Susan Davenport
David Day
Leslie Forbes, Author
Lucy Heller
Mr G Hopkinson
Ian Metherell
Ray Miles
Sasha Moorsom
Malcolm & Liliane Ogden
Paul L Oppenheimer
Clare Rich & Robert Marshall
Martin Shenfield
Ed Smith

Beautiful Things
Anonymous
Anonymous
Mr and Mrs Simon Bass
Alan Brodie
Clive Butler
Clyde Cooper
Patrick and Anne Foster
Albert Fuss
Vivien Goodwin
Ken Griffin
Sheila Hancock
David Hare
Philip Jackson

William Keeling
Adam Kenwright
The Mackintosh Foundation
Laurie Marsh
John Reynolds
Mr and Mrs George Robinson
Tracey Scoffield
Barry Serjent
Brian D Smith
Samuel West
Richard Zajdlic

Glee Club
Anonymous
The Hon Mrs Giancarla Alen-Buckley
Jim Broadbent
Alan Rickman
Shirley Robson
Annette Stone

Lone Star
Princess of Darkness

Bronze Corporate Membership
Act Productions Ltd
Oberon Books Ltd
Working Title Film / WT$_2$

Silver Corporate Membership
The Agency

Platinum Corporate Membership
Anonymous

THE GOD BOTHERERS

First published in this version in 2003 by Oberon Books Ltd.
(incorporating Absolute Classics)
521 Caledonian Road, London N7 9RH
Tel: 020 7607 3637 / Fax: 020 7607 3629

e-mail: oberon.books@btinternet.com
www.oberonbooks.com

A catalogue record for this book is available from the
British Library.

ISBN: 1 84002 415 1

Printed in Great Britain by Antony Rowe Ltd, Chippenham.

Characters

KEITH

IBRAHIMA

LAURA

MONDAY

HARSHA

*Let us stop murdering one another. The earth is not
a lair, neither is it a prison. The earth is a
Paradise, the only one we will ever know.*

Henry Miller, *The Air Conditioned Nightmare*

April

Somewhere in the developing world. The sound of cicadas. The back yard of a Non Governmental Organisation HQ bungalow. It is early evening and the light is beginning to fade. KEITH is listening to The Clash on his headphones and smoking a joint. He is a man of about forty-five wearing shorts and a beach shirt. A muazzin calls the faithful to prayer. Enter IBRAHIMA. She is wearing a burqa with a netted-over eye slit and no flesh showing. She stops before him. He turns his Walkman off. Pause.

KEITH: You look different.

Pause.

The shoes?

IBRAHIMA lifts the burqa to just above the ankle, revealing tarty, gold, strappy high heels. She circles him sensuously, brushing the burqa against him. Then she walks into the bungalow. He takes a swig of beer, stands, and follows her. Enter LAURA. She is twenty-four years old, dressed in GAP fatigues and a MOBY T shirt bearing the slogan EVERYTHING IS WRONG. On the back the T shirt has a list of everything that is wrong – environmental pollution etc. A Gucci hijab covers her head. She is carrying a large travel bag and smaller rucksack bag with a copy of Cosmopolitan *magazine sticking out the back, and a cardboard box covered in customs stickers.*

LAURA: (*Out front.*) Dear Pip, I am here! I am fucking here! Everything is just, like, epic. I am in Tambia or is it 'The' Tambia. Who cares if I'm in the wrong country, I am definitely, definitely not in Burton Latimer. It feels weird writing a letter. I'm gonna die without email. I need my fix! I was stuck in Lakpat for three weeks. Pukesville! Every NGO in, like, the whole world is hanging out in Lakpat, it's just like Uni – 'Shagging sans frontières'. The place is infested with natural blondes, uuuughhh, bastard Scandinavian girls, with their long legs and their long naturally blonde hair, and they are all so fucking tedious, and naturally blonde. Agh!!! Kill, kill, kill! Met a real cute human rights campaigner from New Zealand, half Indian guy, really pretty. He's married. Oh Pip, what is it with me! I'll tell you all about him when I see you. I'm Mad! P.S. Can you send me this week's copy of *Heat*, the one where Nicole Kidman's stuck in a portaloo. I left my copy on the plane. My name's Laura and I'm a *Heat*-aholic. Please write babe!

Enter IBRAHIMA. She is walking swiftly but pauses before LAURA.

(*To IBRAHIMA.*) Allahu Akbar

IBRAHIMA giggles and walks off.

Fuck!

Enter KEITH. He stands upstage of her, watching.

KEITH: You're late.

LAURA: The bus blew a tyre.

KEITH: You're three fucking weeks late.

LAURA: Someone attacked a mosque, riots, hundreds dead. It wasn't my fault. (*Out front.*) I live in a really traditional bungalow thing called an ibi. The design is exactly like all the local indigenous people's houses, except I've got air conditioning, carpets and a toilet. I share the ibi with this guy Keith. The bad news is HE IS MY DAD!

KEITH: Burton Latimer eh? Weetabix.

LAURA: Yeah.

KEITH: Ready Brek – that's a Weetabix product isn't it?

LAURA: I don't know.

KEITH: Do they make Alpen in Burton Latimer?

LAURA: I'm not sure.

KEITH: You do come from Burton Latimer don't you?

LAURA: I worked there. I was born in Sevenoaks.

KEITH: They changed the name of Weetos to Minibix, didn't they? (*Beat.*) Or was it the other way round? Alpen nutty crunch, that's my favourite, can't beat it. Bran, nuts AND it's crunchy.

LAURA: Burton Latimer is fantastically boring, it stinks like a permanent roast dinner, and its population is dedicated to waiting, like, quietly, to die.

KEITH: It's very handy for Kettering.

LAURA: You're just like my dad. Do you like Motorhead? Punk?

KEITH: Motorhead were never punk. They started in seventy-five, which is pre-punk, unless you count the New York Dolls as punk, which I never have. Motorhead were grunge really, but pre-grunge cos grunge was post punk, obviously.

LAURA: (*Laughing.*) I came here to get away from blokes like you.

KEITH: Beer? I know a man, who knows a man, who knows a man. There are not many opportunities for women.

LAURA: Not yet. That's my job! (*Out front.*) When we're not working we're basically, like lashed. We drink, literally, like, tons of this Sun beer.

KEITH: It's a wheat-based German recipe made under licence in Morocco. Nigerian army deserters driving diesel Peugot 405s smuggle it through as far as Lakpat.

It's got added sugar to suit the Tambian taste for sugar. I find it a bit sweet but it's better than a kick in the clems.

LAURA: (*Out front.*) We got drunk the first night, which is kinda risky cos we're living under, like, Sharia Law, yeah? but because we're 'Christians', in inverted commas, we're not like, covered by the same laws as the Muslims who live next door, yeah? It's mad!

KEITH: How the fuck can you expect to run a fucking country when half the fucking laws only apply to half the fucking population!

LAURA: (*Out front.*) I'm not doing VSO, this is an NGO. I get a proper salary. It's a job. Keith's been here three years. He's really positive about the project and the people.

KEITH: It's like herding fucking cats!

LAURA: (*Out front.*) The bus company is run by Christians. It's called 'Death is Certain Buses', and the toilet paper's called 'God is in Control'. Mad!

KEITH: Don't ever say that you don't believe in God, alright? They'll think you're mentally ill. You're Church of England.

LAURA: Cool.

KEITH: And a virgin.

LAURA: I am a virgin.

KEITH: Don't go out without a veil.

LAURA: Actually, it's kinda, liberating –

KEITH: – Crap. (*Beat.*) Wash standing up. Catch the water in a bucket so we can flush the loo. When I was in the Philippines, 86, 87 we used to shit in the jungle. You had to take a spade with you, not to dig a hole, but to kill the snakes.

LAURA: 'Luxury'.

KEITH: I watched an NPA platoon kill a Filipino peasant with a spade. They could have shot him but with a spade you can all have a go.

LAURA: Couldn't you have stopped it?

KEITH: We were there to find alternatives to burning rice straw. Environmentally catastrophic. (*Beat.*) Don't wash out here. The boys poked holes in the fence. Victoria.

LAURA: She came home early, didn't she? Something about er… –

KEITH: – She got pissed at the army barracks and then, watched by fifty soldiers, half the kpelle, and me, she gave a German Aids Awareness Outreach worker a blow job in the car park.

LAURA: I'll try and remember not to do that then.

KEITH: She's gone back to live in Goole. She's training to be a drama therapist.

Enter MONDAY. He's a Tambian of about twenty-five wearing torn shorts, a blue fez, flip flops and a T shirt which says DIP ME IN HONEY AND THROW ME TO THE LESBIANS.

You're the only white woman for three hundred square miles so you get a twenty-four hour guard, a mimani.

LAURA: Is that, like, totally necessary?

KEITH: Completely unnecessary. It's not Belle Yella.

LAURA: I hope not. Oh God! They're all shitting themselves about Belle Yella in Bracknell.

KEITH: (*To MONDAY.*) You're late!

MONDAY: I collided with a huge python in the road and nearly got bitten.

KEITH: You're lying!

MONDAY: The python was hopping mad!

KEITH: You've been drinking!

MONDAY: I was thrown off my pukpuk and didn't know what to do! I thought my days of cheese were over! Then I remembered the words of Richard Nixon – 'defeat is never fatal unless you give up'. So I fell to my knees and prayed to that gentleman of Nazareth and BANG!, along comes the money truck from the Central Bank and runs over the python's head! The rest, as they say, is history.

KEITH: You're drunk.

MONDAY: I am going to divorce booze and marry Christ! (*To LAURA.*) I will be a great mimani, maybe the greatest ever. I have studied the habits of lions. You will not be killed – over my dead body!

LAURA: Hi. Laura.

LAURA puts her hand out to shake.

MONDAY: Oh no!

KEITH: In this province a man can't touch a woman.

MONDAY: Don't start! Or we might as well have it off and all go back to mini skirts!

LAURA: (*Out front.*) Monday is, like, a Missionary name, but he's a Muslim, but, oh God, it's, like, really complicated.

MONDAY: I was born a Muslim, but in the orphanage Jesus Christ came to me one night when I was playing Scrabble and made me his lifelong friend.

LAURA: Right.

MONDAY: I am also technically Jewish, but that was a clerical error. I am circumcised, and a very poor job they did too. I could have done better myself.

LAURA: O.K.

MONDAY: It is a great sense of shame to me that I cannot pee straight.

LAURA: Sure, yeah.

MONDAY: I am Kebbe and follow the Poro religion.

LAURA: Poro?

MONDAY: Oh yes! I have the big three – Christian, Muslim, and Poro. Manchester United, Arsenal, and Chelsea.

LAURA: Right.

MONDAY: I am also a witch, but we can leave that for a rainy day.

LAURA: (*To KEITH.*) I thought it was like, pretty much all Muslim round here.

KEITH: Poro and Muslim round here, Sunni Muslim that is; Poro and Christian five miles south, and pockets of Shia Muslim and Poro all over the place. Everyone's Poro, except the women, who are Sande, which is the same as Poro but just another name because they're women.

MONDAY: Doesn't matter because my God is all the same man!

LAURA: Or woman. (*To KEITH quickly.*) Sorry!

MONDAY: Oh yes! Equal rights for women! I am a very modern thinking mimani, very western. God, oh yes, 'she' is bloody everywhere! Or he. But definitely not gay.

KEITH: This is the traditional hat of a Christian from the Egwome clan. His drinking hat.

MONDAY: My brother, Ifeamyi, calls me Mr. Weakling! He is a fully qualified pharmacist. He has three wives and eleven sons. He is a good Muslim, he never drinks. One day I will ask him how he does it!

KEITH: (*Kicks the can of water.*) How much?

MONDAY: (*To KEITH.*) Two hundred doss! Full to the brim, no piss.

KEITH: Twenty doss.

MONDAY: (*Laughs hysterically.*) Look, it is not red water. One hundred and fifty.

KEITH: Twenty five.

MONDAY: At the bore hole, many hungry lions, much hiding, many clever things.

KEITH: Forty.

MONDAY: Fifty.

MONDAY/KEITH: Forty-five.

KEITH hands over some notes, MONDAY counts them, and pockets them.

MONDAY: Today we have a new Imam. Ali Bakassa. He is a student from the city.

KEITH: Oh shit!

MONDAY: Ha, ha! He is just a boy with a very short beard, but holy Moses, what a student! We are all instructed to stop our wives working in the Casino.

KEITH: You don't have a wife.

MONDAY: If I had a wife she would have to resign today!

KEITH: They pay well.

MONDAY: Do they? Oh bugger, we could do with the money!

KEITH takes the jerry can into the ibi.

(*To LAURA.*) I am saving up for a twenty cow wife.

LAURA: Right! Would your wife be, like, a Muslim?

MONDAY: Oh yes! She would be very much like a Muslim, in fact she would be a Muslim.

LAURA: I think Islam, I mean, the whole veil thing, is actually, like, a way of showing real respect for women. 'Real respect', yeah? Not like women are treated in the west, like, in the porn industry, you know what I mean?

MONDAY: Oh yes! Christians think a Muslim beats his wife up black and blue, and cuts her ears off if she has a girl child, and of course, I'm not saying that doesn't happen, but there is no instruction anywhere in the Koran for behaving like a mad gorilla. No! The Prophet Muhammad, peace be upon him, never beat a single woman in the whole of his life, never! Not that anyone knows about anyway.

LAURA: Absolutely.

MONDAY: Islam is the top religion. Except Shi'a Muslims. They're all coconut heads.

KEITH: (*Off.*) He's Sunni.

LAURA: There's two sorts of Muslim aren't there, Sunni, and Shia, and then there's the Sufis. I'm reading the Koran.

MONDAY: It's unputdownable isn't it?

KEITH re-enters.

KEITH: Oi! Take these bags through.

MONDAY picks up the bags, taking an interest in the Cosmo, *and takes them into the ibi.*

I'm gonna do a big Christmas dinner. Turkey. All the trimmings.

LAURA: What now? It's May.

KEITH: At Christmas. I am actually a Christian. Relax, it's not a heavy thing, O.K. Are you gonna be here at Christmas?

LAURA: Here or John Lewis's. Here.

KEITH: Great. Is this mine?

KEITH opens a package which LAURA has brought with her. It's got customs stickers all over it.

Did customs want a dash?

LAURA: I, like, refused at first. But then they got really heavy. Said my malaria tablets had a heroin content, which is true, of course, pain killer yeah?

KEITH: A thousand?

KEITH takes out a battery operated drill and inspects it.

LAURA: Fifteen hundred.

KEITH: Not bad!

LAURA: It does my head in. I, like, love the developing world yeah, I travelled in my gap year, Africa, South America, Nepal. Yam foo foo is, like, my all time favourite meal. I'm a giraffe girl. My dad always bought me little cuddly giraffes. But the one thing I'd change – bribes.

KEITH: That's the one thing you'd change about Tambia?

LAURA: Yes. And aids of course, and poverty, and famine.

KEITH: Your training plan is fucked.

LAURA: Three weeks late?

KEITH: I have to go to Kante in the morning. I'll be gone about a month.

LAURA: Oh God.

KEITH: Have you got a pen? This country's fucked, alright. Write that down.

LAURA writes it down, KEITH waits.

The borders don't make sense, the capital is on the coast, which is no fucking use to anyone, there's no rule of law, no running water, you never know when the electric's on, the last war's fucked everything, and the next war will fuck everything else.

LAURA: When does the next war start?

KEITH: January the third. The beards will win the elections again, but the government will reject the result again saying, that an Islamic administration would not be in the long term interests of Tambia, ie: not in the short term interests of Exxon Mobil, Chevron Texaco, Elf Aquitaine and any other oil companies who Tambia's self-serving fucking kleptocracy, also known as the People's Movement for Democractic Reform, are in bed with, or should I say, 'being shafted up the arse by'.

LAURA: Kleptocracy. That's your word isn't it.

KEITH: Nobody has any loyalty to Tambia as a nation state cos they're all Kebbe first, or whatever their tribe is; they're Muslim or Christian second; and only ever fucking Tambian when the football team's on telly.

LAURA: But the people are really, you know, so fantastic aren't they, I mean –

KEITH: – Crap. It's a male-dominated, tradition-oriented, patriarchal society ie: it's fucked. In three years I haven't met a single Tambian who could organise a fart in an arsehole. Do you think I swear too much?

LAURA: No. It shows a, you know, passion for er…justice.

KEITH: 'A lot of people won't get no justice tonight.' The Clash. The Clash are one of the two reasons I'm here.

LAURA: What's the other? You're a Christian. My dad quite likes the Clash. His favourite band is Steely Dan.

KEITH looks at her with contempt.

KEITH: What did they tell you about me in Bracknell?

LAURA: Good things. They kinda warned me that you swear a lot.

KEITH: Peter fucking Nicholson eh? (*Beat.*) He could wank for England. What's your favourite band?

LAURA: Er…I don't really…The White Stripes? Actually, my really favourite band is Radiohead. I forgot.

KEITH: (*Evangelical.*) I saw the Clash twenty-three times.

Picking a CD from his package.

Is this new Strokes album any good?

LAURA: I don't know.

KEITH: (*Reading the back of the CD.*) Fucking hell, thirty three minutes, is that all we get? Kaw! Do you remember Sandinista. Triple album. Six sides of vinyl. That's two CDs to you.

LAURA: The oil boom must have made a difference?

KEITH: Yeah, there's a new drug. Megwe. Megwe is cloth dipped in diesel. Chew it and it eliminates hunger pangs.

LAURA: Right.

KEITH chucks over some thick documents to LAURA as he talks.

KEITH: Proclamation 35/97. Government statement on Micro finance initiatives. Proclamation 39/99 National Micro and Small Enterprises Development Strategy. Muslim women can't capitalise their businesses cos they've got no collateral and paying interest is haram. Haram?

LAURA: Yeah, er…halal good, haram er…not good, bad even. I'm reading the Koran, I thought I'd –

KEITH: – how far have you got?

LAURA: I'm up to the bit where…page four.

KEITH: (*Chucking down a document.*) Here's your girls, they're mostly war widows. It's basic stuff, you don't need an MBA.

LAURA: That's lucky!

KEITH: Improve productivity. Cut costs. Find new markets. Who's the first?

LAURA: Omojola hairdressing.

KEITH: Three women, fuck knows how many kids running about, one pair of scissors, no running water, no work ethic and no fucking mirror.

LAURA: Right.

KEITH: They can't cut men's hair cos women can't touch men. So they're left with boys, which is not enough of a market to feed three families.

LAURA: Why don't they cut women's hair?

KEITH: Women like to have their hair cut properly.

LAURA: So, er…training and er…electric clippers. Hand clippers!

KEITH: And a mirror.

LAURA: Three mirrors!

KEITH: Good, like it. And signage.

LAURA: Signage?

KEITH: A board outside.

LAURA: Oh signage!

KEITH: They don't want to pay their sign board taxes. They need to establish 'personal contact with influential officials'.

LAURA: I have to encourage them to pay a bribe?

KEITH: What did Peter fucking Nicholson teach you in Bracknell?

LAURA: Work 'in' the culture, and 'with' the culture, not 'against' the culture.

KEITH: If you fly club class, you're paying a bribe in order to be treated like a human being rather than a mollusc with short legs. Poverty is the enemy. Not culture. What's the enemy?

LAURA: You just said.

KEITH: Yeah, poverty and ignorance. Most of these businesses are in the villages around Unoka, none of them are on the phone. You ride a motorbike don't you?

LAURA: Yes.

KEITH: I'm gonna bed. Early start. Difficult shit with the French. I am this far away from dragging Unoka into the nineteenth century. A tap. One fucking tap.

LAURA: Good luck.

KEITH: Good night. (*Out front.*) The Diesel Boys. Four of them, dressed in red, Ferrari red, Michael Schumachers. The motorbikes are aerosol can sprayed red. Sunglasses, AK 47s, flip flops. It's Friday, and the Shi'a faithful are at prayer. The boys riding pillion kick off their flip flops. They're Muslims too. Sunni. Allahu Akbar. They fire, reload, fire, reload, fire and leave. Thirty two dead. Riots, curfew. Six hundred, maybe a thousand dead. The Christians working on Casino island are cut off, too scared to cross the bridge. A journalist for the *Daily Telegraph* notices that the staff of the French water company Vivendi Environment now travel in armed convoy. She identifies their security guards' rifles as FA MAS 5.56 millimeter assault rifles, the standard issue rifle of the French foreign legion. Jacques Chirac denies he has sent government troops. The journalist is arrested and deported. The *Daily Telegraph* pigs out on indignation. On the London Underground *Independent* and *Guardian* readers pick up discarded *Telegraphs* and are surprised and impressed by the quality of the writing. And Peter fucking Nicholson in his safe european home sends me a fucking idiot.

KEITH exits to the ibi. It is now dark, and there are bird and animal noises above the cicadas. Enter MONDAY. He is distributing lion turds around the compound.

LAURA: What's that?

MONDAY: Lion poo!

LAURA: Right.

MONDAY: Imagine you are a little runty leopard and you have the big idea – 'let's go eat the new whitey girl!' So! You nip over the fence but then you see this big lion poo sausage here and you say, Allah be merciful! That is one big fuck off lion! Let's go home now! (*Beat.*) You see, I am clever, like an old fish.

LAURA: Do you have a gun?

MONDAY: I can get you one.

LAURA: No, I'm just not used to, like, everyone you see is carrying a gun.

MONDAY: You will not die tonight. Over my dead body!

LAURA: D you stay awake all night?

MONDAY: I listen to the world service. It is beautiful.

MONDAY winds up one of those self-generating radios and we hear Melvyn Bragg talking about epistemology.

To black.

May

IBRAHIMA sucking from a can of diet Pepsi with a straw. Enter LAURA from the road in a veil and carrying post. A fresh water can.

LAURA: (*Out front.*) Dear Pip. You haven't written! Did Trish go ahead and marry Theo? Everyone knows Trish is shagging Damien. Everyone but Theo. Doooh! I have to wear a veil. The veil is all about not getting the men sexually excited, and that's really sensible, isn't it, and yet another thing to respect about Islam. I bought a classic hijab in the duty free at Heathrow. It's plain charcoal with very small, very subtle Guccis all over it. I'm reading 'The Idiot's Guide to Islam'. It's such an amazing peaceful, loving religion and all those terrorists, they're not really Muslims at all it's kinda media shorthand. I mean, we would never describe Fred West or Adolf Hitler as 'christians'. We would never say 'the Christian fascist', although he was a Christian, and a vegetarian actually, Hitler I mean, not Fred West – he was a builder. First day at work and I've never ever talked to a woman in a burqa and I've never been any good at small talk. Go for it!

IBRAHIMA gurgles on her straw.

(*To IBRAHIMA.*) And stoning, yeah, well, you know, how is that any worse than the electric chair, yeah?

IBRAHIMA gurgles on her straw.

In America, yeah, which is fundamentalist Christian now, yeah, well, the state executes poor black people all the time, Afro Americans.

IBRAHIMA gurgles on her straw.

I know they don't, like, execute you for, you know, sleeping with someone you're not married to, but it's all value judgements, and there is no such thing as an absolute morality. We did that at Uni.

IBRAHIMA gurgles on her straw.

Your culture values family, and promiscuity is a threat, so getting heavy with anyone who threatens the culture is, like, understandable cos the first responsibility of any culture is for its own survival.

IBRAHIMA gurgles on her straw.

Do you have to do that? My sister used to do that. The thought of all that flob in the bottom of the can – ugh. Sorry.

IBRAHIMA: Why are you not married?

LAURA: Me? I have nothing against marriage as a concept, or kids. The survival of the species is what it's all about in the end, and everything else is, like, self-indulgent really, yeah? So, kids, yes, definitely. But not just yet.

IBRAHIMA: Your father must have a big farm.

LAURA: He's not a farmer. He's a cat plate artist. He paints cats onto plates. He went to art school with David Bowie? And he teaches.

IBRAHIMA: What does he teach?

LAURA: Cat plate art. What I would say though, and I realise I'm out of order here, – I think if you have to stone the woman, you should stone the man too. I'm not a feminist, no I mean, men are, like, important, still, particularly over here, you know, where there's still a lot of lifting. The turnover of the American porn industry is bigger than Zambia's GDP. So, you have three daughters. Are they at school?

IBRAHIMA: I don't want them to go to school.

LAURA: I respect that. One of the first things they taught us at Bracknell was that's it's so important to accept Tambia –

IBRAHIMA: – Tambekistan.

LAURA: Sorry! Tambekistan. Weird that isn't it, you know, having a different name for the country cos you're a woman? Not weird for you of course because you live here. It's so easy to talk to you. There are so many misconceptions about the veil. Do you love your husband, or was it an arranged marriage?

IBRAHIMA: My father, and him, made an agreement.

LAURA: Of course. *Daily Mail* readers, stupid people, they always think an arranged marriage is like a licence for the husband to hit his wife. But your husband doesn't beat you does he?

IBRAHIMA: Yes.

LAURA: Any particular reason?

IBRAHIMA: I give him only girls.

LAURA: O.K.

IBRAHIMA: I am pregnant again.

LAURA: Congratulations! I mean, oh shit.

IBRAHIMA starts crying.

Don't cry. Please.

IBRAHIMA: I must wait until the eighth month before I can go to the Earth Spirit. She will decide if it is to be a boy.

LAURA: Is that Poro stuff?

IBRAHIMA: Sande. I am a woman.

LAURA: Right. But you're a Muslim as well?

IBRAHIMA: The Earth spirit did not leave when Muhammad came.

LAURA: Peace be upon him.

Enter MONDAY reading LAURA's Cosmopolitan.

MONDAY: (*Turning pages of* Cosmopolitan.) Skinny! Skinny! Very skinny, ha, ha! (*Turning the pages again.*) Skinny. Skinny. Skinny.

LAURA: Sorry, that's my magazine.

MONDAY: I was hoping to find a nice fat woman!

IBRAHIMA: Kwa coche, phut, phut, phut.

MONDAY: (*Shouting.*) Umeooa! Kwa shumo! Konde!

MONDAY puts the magazine down. IBRAHIMA picks it up and leaves.

IBRAHIMA: (*To MONDAY.*) Yazid! Coche!

MONDAY: Fornicator!

IBRAHIMA: Phut, phut, phut. (*Giggles.*)

LAURA: Please!

MONDAY: (*To IBRAHIMA.*) There is no history of fornication in my family! (*To LAURA.*) They call us the iron family!

MONDAY sticks two fingers up at IBRAHIMA then taps the can.

LAURA: Thank you!

MONDAY: Water. Today – big thirsty rhino. Three hundred doss.

LAURA: Er…two hundred doss.

MONDAY: Ha, ha! No, no you say thirty.

LAURA: Thirty doss.

MONDAY: Thirty!? Are you crazy woman!

LAURA: Why can't you just have, like, a set price?

MONDAY: Every can of water in Tambia is different. Today it is hot, sticky, and my puk puk has a plastic seat.

LAURA: Fifty.

MONDAY: One hundred.

LAURA: Ninety.

LAURA/MONDAY: Eighty-five.

They involuntarily shake hands.

MONDAY: Now we are both happy and my heart is a bullock of joy!

LAURA: No touching.

LAURA counts out money.

MONDAY: Also, I sell anything Russian. Kalashnikovs, second hand heart attack defibrillators, Pringles.

LAURA: Vodka?

MONDAY: I will get you vodka, but you must not be friendly with 'Fornicator'. She has converted her legs into business premises.

LAURA: She's a prostitute?

MONDAY: She is useless to her husband! But I am not a Mary Whitehouse! NO! God tells us that sex is good, very good! And I have no intention of spending my life hiding behind the curtains, but fornication is the work of the devil!

LAURA: You will soon have a twenty cow wife.

MONDAY: Or two ten cow wives.

LAURA: You can have three wives can't you.

MONDAY: Two is enough. Three in a bed and you can still be romantic. Four is just a mad olympics!

LAURA: Right. Monday, advice, the post. Am I supposed to open it?

MONDAY: (*Laughing.*) You are asking me?!

LAURA: I'll open everything addressed to the project, yeah?

MONDAY: I am the mimani!

LAURA: (*Inspecting the postmark.*) It's addressed to Keith. CSA Oldham. Is Keith married?

MONDAY: He has two wives. Two 'money grabbing bitches'.

LAURA: Right. Let's go. I lied on my application form. I can't ride a motorbike.

MONDAY: No?! You are grade five piano aren't you?

LAURA: Did I put that? If you ride the motorbike I'll put my arms round you. I've done that before.

MONDAY: You are always trying to touch me!

LAURA: How do you get anything done in this country if there's no touching?!

MONDAY: You can sit behind me in my puk puk box.

LAURA: People will think I'm your wife.

MONDAY grins.

To black.

June

KEITH is reading project reports. LAURA is down stage with a handful of photographs.

LAURA: (*Out front.*) Dear Pip. Trish looks such a tart! She might be wearing white but you can see her nipples! And what is that tattoo? It looks like a lamb chop! Your hair! You're gorgeous! You look like Debbie Harry, you know, when she was young and still on heroin. I've learnt to ride a motorbike – see photo. But where's my *Heat* magazine. I just need some 'Courtney Love wins the Miss Cellulite competition in at China White.' This isn't VSO. I work for an NGO. It's a job. It's been a totally incredible month and my clients, the women, are fantastic, dignified, unbelievable. I just hope I'm helping, they giggle so much I get paranoid, and then I can't sleep for worrying about whether they can feed their kids. I realise now how incredibly important my work is. (*To KEITH.*) Did you get your post?

KEITH: No.

LAURA goes into the ibi.

Who is Lookout Masulu?

LAURA: (*From the window of her room.*) P.S. I've met someone Pip. He's Tambian. Black. Sorry! If you shut your eyes he could be English. He did media studies at Southampton Institute. He looks like Seal, but with good skin. He works for Tambia Cell. More people have aids in Tambia than have mobile phones. He's married. I'm just so 'the other woman'. Four stars, occasionally five. Older men! They are such better drivers!

KEITH: (*To himself.*) Lookout Masulu.

LAURA gives KEITH two items of post, both A4-size serious looking envelopes. Pause during which LAURA expects KEITH to open his post and share it. He looks at her.

LAURA: Sorry! I'm so desperate for post myself, I –

KEITH: (*Looking at first envelope.*) – Child support agency –

LAURA: – No, it's O.K. Sorry.

KEITH: (*Looking at second envelope.*) And decree nisi, hopefully.

LAURA: That's really pants of me!

KEITH: If it is we'll have a celebration drink.

LAURA: I apologise.

KEITH: Don't. I spent all of 1993 up to my knees in shit in Cambodia. Literally, it was a sewage project. She spent the whole year in bed with an award-winning butcher from Pateley Bridge. (*Ignoring the post, going back to the project reports.*) Lookout Masulu, Lookout Masulu. Who the fucking hell is Lookout Masulu?

LAURA: He's, like, the contracts manager at Tambia cell.

KEITH: All your girls have got mobile fucking phones!?

LAURA: Not all of them.

Enter IBRAHIMA, talking on a mobile.

IBRAHIMA: Eeeee! Agi kwondo…agi…agi. Eeeeee! Ik kom kwefi gim, agi!

IBRAHIMA off into the ibi.

KEITH: What the fuck has been going on here?!

LAURA: None of the villages had any telecoms, yeah? Lookout gave me fifty phones.

KEITH: 'Gave?'

LAURA: They're leased. My girls charge the user about a hundred percent mark up per call. It's like every village having a public phone. People check out the price of milk or beans in the markets, save themselves a trip, or go to a different market, where they get a better price. I've fucked up haven't I?

KEITH: I've been trying to get Tambia Telecom to commission an exchange for three fucking years, but every time they put a bit of cable in the ground it gets dug up and nicked.

LAURA: Didn't you consider mobiles?

KEITH: How do they recharge the batteries?

LAURA: Little solar panels.

KEITH: They're expensive.

LAURA: I started a credit club. They can borrow ten thousand doss at seven percent interest, and pay it back over a year.

KEITH: They're Muslims. They can't pay interest.

LAURA: They don't pay interest. They pay the bank a bill for financial consultancy, the equivalent of interest.

KEITH: That's crap. The bank would never go for that.

LAURA: I had to pay him a dash.

KEITH: You're very lateral aren't you?

LAURA: Fish!

KEITH: Where did you get the idea of getting into bed with Tambia Cell?

LAURA: I don't know. It just came to me.

KEITH: We tried this kinda collective use thing in Gaza in 82. Worked well, for a while.

LAURA: (*Hugely disappointed.*) Oh.

KEITH: They were all communists in them days.

LAURA: The Palestinians?

KEITH: Yeah. When the soviet union went tits up, they swapped their clapped out red flag for a nice shiny green one.

LAURA: Have you spent your whole life in, like, development work?

KEITH: Yeah. Pretty much.

LAURA: Are we getting a tap then?

KEITH: Huh, long story. The Tambian official has been off for two months because his cousin's poorly. Not 'his mother's dying', or 'his father's having a complete fucking skeleton transplant', but 'his cousin is poorly'. You're supposed to hate your fucking cousins! You want them to die!

LAURA: We're getting a tap aren't we?

KEITH: Next month.

LAURA: Fantastic! A tap!

She hugs him.

Enter MONDAY. He watches with open jealousy.

KEITH: That's been a pretty long Friday prayers?

MONDAY: Today we must seek out any women human rights workers and marry them on the spot! That way they will all get a bun in the oven and will spend the rest of their lives indoors!

KEITH: The student with the short beard?

MONDAY: It is growing at a phenomenal pace. Either God is with him or he's using anabolic steroids. I listen to the world service. (*To LAURA.*) Will you marry me?

KEITH laughs.

LAURA: I'm not a human rights worker.

KEITH: How many cows?

MONDAY: She is old, like a big tree.

LAURA: I'm twenty-four.

KEITH: Come on, how many cows?

LAURA: I don't want any cows.

MONDAY: Are you a virgin?

LAURA: I am a virgin.

MONDAY: Off the mark with five cows! Are you open or closed?

LAURA: (*Not knowing what he's talking about.*) I'm not… open, I'm shut, I think.

MONDAY: Closed. Did they sew you up nice and neat or is it all to cock?

KEITH: She's not been circumcised.

MONDAY: That is so English! You spoil the ship for a ha'porth of tar!

KEITH: A Muslim girl who hasn't been spayed gets a low bride price.

LAURA: I'm sorry, but you're wrong O.K? FGM has got absolutely nothing to do with Islam.

KEITH: FGM?

LAURA: Female Genital Mutilation. It's common in Christian countries like Kenya, too. It's a cultural tradition which, like, totally pre-dates Islam.

MONDAY: Very popular though! Especially with the ladies!

LAURA: Yeah, because women are, like, disempowered. Don't look at me like that. I haven't read the Koran, but I can't imagine Mohammed –

MONDAY: – peace be upon him –

LAURA: – peace be upon him, yeah, er…where was I?

MONDAY: Mohammed, peace be upon him.

LAURA: Yes, I can't imagine Mohammed –

MONDAY: – Peace be upon him –

LAURA: Yes, alright, just don't do that. (*Louder.*) I can't imagine… –

KEITH: – Him.

LAURA: Him being in favour of it.

MONDAY: He said 'if you cut, do not overdo it, because it brings more radiance to the face and it is more pleasant for the husband.'

KEITH: Know thine enemy.

LAURA: I'm sorry! Who's my enemy?

KEITH: Anyhow, she hasn't been FGM'd so what does that make her worth?

MONDAY: Two cows.

LAURA: I've got a first in Business Studies from Loughborough University.

MONDAY: One cow. (*To KEITH.*) But have you heard? Every village has a cell phone!

KEITH: I know.

MONDAY: Great Britain is still sticking up telegraph poles. Ha, ha! Tambia is now the lion, and England is a wildebeest with a limp.

KEITH: We are in the middle of a meeting.

MONDAY: She learnt to ride a motorbike very quick!

A sharp glance from KEITH to LAURA.

KEITH: Monday!

MONDAY: They all love her! Lemonade Fatima, you know the one you fancy, the one with the arse? She now has ice!

KEITH: Ice?!

MONDAY: Oh yes! Laura told that arab bugger in the bakery to let Fatima use a corner of his big fuck off gas industrial freezer!

LAURA: For a little dash.

MONDAY: And Mahjabeen?

KEITH: What about Mahji?

MONDAY: Laura goes straight in there! Ha! 'Mahjabeen, your mats are crap! No bugger wants your crap mats!' Mahji borrows the money, buys a Singer sewing machine, beautiful, and is now mending torn curtains.

LAURA: The hotels on Casino island always have torn curtains.

MONDAY: From their wild and sinful nights.

KEITH: You went to the island?

LAURA: We took all the girls from the pottery out there and sold nearly seventy night light pots. Night lights, like candles, yeah.

KEITH: I know what night lights are.

MONDAY: They have taught her to dance. Show him! Go and get the fornicator, you can dance with her, show him how you dance.

LAURA exits to the ibi.

She is a one woman locust storm! But very skinny.

KEITH: She's not gonna marry you. Look, I go home after Christmas, Laura stays for maybe another year. In the long term you're gonna need to find some kinda alternative income.

MONDAY: I will go to America and be big in motor parts!

KEITH: When I was in Mali in 1985, I was leaning against a three ton maize crib sharing a joint with a bloke when he said 'why is the maize in this maize crib fucking rotten'. Yeah, he swore. He was angry. He was Bob Geldof. For eighteen years now I've been thinking about what he said and I've noticed that the big maize cribs round here are exactly the same design as those in Mali. Design a maize crib where the cobs on the bottom don't rot and you could make a living as a joiner.

MONDAY: I know the Kebbe. They will never pay money for something they can do themselves.

KEITH: You're on my payroll. Think about it, talk to farmers, do a design. Homework. Yeah, Geldof. Boomtown Rats. Kaw! 'I don't like Mondays.' He wouldn't like you.

Simple music is played by IBRAHIMA and LAURA, they dance on, LAURA is in a light coloured burqua, and, during the next they do the dance.

KEITH: I've seen this dance before.

MONDAY: Yes, it is the dance to celebrate the joys of female circumcision.

KEITH: Oh that one.

MONDAY: It is soon to be the festival of the day of the longest sun.

KEITH: Clitoridectomy day.

The dance ends. They applaud.

MONDAY: This year it will be different. There will be many tourists.

KEITH: What?

MONDAY: Laura has made many clever deals with tour operators. Many buses! It will be like a white horse Wembley!

KEITH: Tourists want to see a big black bloke prancing about like a deranged acid casualty, caked in cow shit, with a dead chicken nailed to his head. They don't want to see nine year old girls getting butchered!

MONDAY: We will sell many nick nacks.

To black.

July

LAURA is crouched puking.

KEITH: I hear it went well.

LAURA: (*Quietly.*) Fuck off.

KEITH: (*Laughs.*) Three buses. Japanese, Germans and –

LAURA: – Fuck off!

KEITH: Is it still those two old women? Laurel and Hardy?

LAURA: Leave me alone.

KEITH: How about Miss World next year?

LAURA: Fuck off.

Exit KEITH.

(*Out front, through pukes.*) Dear Pip, Everything is going really well here. I'm really enjoying it. It is difficult sometimes because you have to constantly remind yourself that what you value, the things you believe in – (*Pukes.*) Stephanie?! *I* introduced Damien to Stephie. She won't stick him long, he's such a two-star shag. I've had a council tax reminder from Hackney Council, which is weird, cos I've never lived in Hackney. P.S. *Heat!* P.P.S. My mimani, Monday has got the hots for me. He's sweet, but he's so innocent.

MONDAY: Will you marry me?

LAURA: Who's got my *Cosmo*?

MONDAY: I have many powers. I am a witch don't forget.

LAURA: What? You could, like, make me marry you?

MONDAY: Yes. I walked out of the forest, two days old, trailing my cord behind me, singing 'God Save the Queen' in Welsh!

LAURA: I want my *Cosmo* back. Now!

MONDAY: Only a witch could do that. It's a very difficult language – Welsh.

LAURA: Your parents made that witch story up! They had twelve children already. The whole witch thing round here is about poverty, that's the first thing they taught us in Bracknell. Your parents called you a witch so they could abandon you. You're not a witch!

Exit MONDAY, shocked.

Oh shit! Monday! Monday! Come back!

LAURA follows him.

(*Off.*) Monday!

IBRAHIMA enters from the ibi. She is reading Cosmopolitan *and is on the phone.*

IBRAHIMA: (*On the phone. Reading/giggling.*) Eeeee! Agi, agi. Cho kwole wa. 'Women instigate sex forty-seven percent of the time…' (*Giggles.*) '… an earth-moving fifty-two percent tell their lovers exactly what to do to make them come…' (*Giggles.*). 'Thanks to *Cosmopolitan* women are enjoying luxurious and aspirational sex.' Eeee! Agi. Kwa?… 'Tips? Games?' (*She turns a page.*) 'American hot pizza! A chilli-pepper-hot role-play game guaranteed to deliver extra pepperoni! Tell your man to go out and get a pizza. He must dress in pizza delivery boy clothes, if he's got a Honda 50 all the better. Whilst he's gone, dress in your most sensuous – '

Enter LAURA.

IBRAHIMA rings off, guiltily.

LAURA: You've got it!

IBRAHIMA: I was reading about Mary Robinson.

LAURA: What?

IBRAHIMA: She was running Ireland and the United Nations and she's got three children.

LAURA: Oh her. Yes. Very impressive. Did you read the sex survey?

IBRAHIMA: No. I like looking at the cars for women. Muslim women are allowed to drive in England?

LAURA: Definitely, yes, there's absolutely no discrimination.

IBRAHIMA: That could be very dangerous if they're wearing the full burqa.

LAURA: Maybe not big lorries.

IBRAHIMA: Can I borrow it?

LAURA: No! It's, like, puerile, crap. I only bought it for...I normally buy *Marie Claire.*

IBRAHIMA: I'm half way through reading about the whore. She has two daughters –

LAURA: She's not a whore, she's a lap dancer? She has an autistic child! How can you say that. I'm not judging you. O.K. But you were judging the lap dancer. A friend of mine did a porn shoot once in Mexico.

IBRAHIMA: You? Your friend is you.

LAURA: I'm not ashamed of it. It was really quite celebratory, you know, of the female form, and it paid for my flight to Rio, yeah? I know about you and Keith.

IBRAHIMA: Keith is a generous man and a good lover.

LAURA: Really?

IBRAHIMA: Oh yes. He's very quick.

LAURA: Is there any chance that Keith is the father of your child?

IBRAHIMA: He wears a rubber.

Enter KEITH. He goes to get a beer, comes back with two.

Can I borrow it please?

LAURA: I can't lend it to you.

KEITH: Oh go on.

LAURA: But –

KEITH: Read it! Memorise it!

IBRAHIMA goes into the ibi with the magazine.

LAURA: Peter Nicholson said –

KEITH: – Peter who?

LAURA: Peter 'fucking' Nicholson said we should avoid –

KEITH: – Her sister used to clean at the refinery apartments. She used to pick the *Playboys* out of the bins, pass them on to Ibrahima who would sell them to me. What? Two thousand Tambians go to University in the West each year. What do you think they bring back? HP sauce?

LAURA: I dunno.

KEITH: In 1993 I was living with the Irrawaddy river indians, Myanmar yeah? Burma?

LAURA: Burma, yeah.

KEITH: They had electric guitars. No shoes, no schools, no hospitals. Electric guitars. No electricity. I taught them reggae. Is that wrong?

LAURA: What were you supposed to be doing there?

KEITH: I can't remember.

KEITH sits.

LAURA: Did you get your post?

KEITH: Letter from Denise.

LAURA: Does all your salary go straight to the bank then?

KEITH: It goes into my bank, hangs around for five minutes, then disappears again into her bank and the other half into Pauline's. My wife. I never see any of it.

LAURA: You live off your Tambian allowance then?

KEITH: Yup. Without that ten quid a week I'd be fucked.

LAURA: Have you got a good job to go back to?

KEITH: Part-time lecturing. I'm not a graduate. Development studies. It's not the job. I miss the kids. I want to be a dad.

LAURA: Not a husband?

KEITH: We'll get married.

LAURA: Have you got a house?

KEITH: No. Pauline's got my house. D's got a decent place. Small but everywhere's small when there's kids.

LAURA: What's the letter?

KEITH: Our Jacob's getting bullied at school.

LAURA: Do all your kids have biblical names?

KEITH: They're very popular nowadays.

LAURA: How many kids are getting called Herod?

KEITH: There's a renewed interest in God.

LAURA: My sister's had her daughter christened so she could go to a Catholic school. They're not even Catholics. She says the school is a 'good' school. Her husband's more honest, he said 'is the Pope a Paki?'

(*Beat.*) I was abused on a Christian outwardboundy kinda thing. The instructor poured hot cocoa down my arm?

KEITH: They used to whack us with hurley sticks.

LAURA: That's Irish isn't it.

KEITH: Manchester Church of England Reform School.

LAURA: Is that like borstal?

KEITH: Special school. I used to steal bikes. You worked as well as studied. Half God half punishment. I made a lot of mattresses, sprung mattresses. I ran away when I was thirteen.

LAURA: Did they abuse you, you know, sexually? Sorry.

KEITH: Not me. Just beatings. The nuns were the worst. We used to call them the sisters of Mussolini.

(*Beat.*) Where's Monday?

LAURA: He…er…went off. In a bit of a huff. I said I didn't think he was a witch.

KEITH: (*Laughs.*)

LAURA: It's not funny. Where will he have gone?

KEITH: Which hat did he have on?

LAURA: His drinking hat.

To black.

August

KEITH and LAURA sit. They have a bottle of vodka between them. It is evening. KEITH is reading the Idiot's Guide to Islam.

LAURA: (*Out front.*) Dear Pip, I'm drunk. We now have a tap in the village! It's totally, totally fantastic! The women used to have to spend five hours a day walking to the bore hole. I've enclosed a photo of the tap. I saw a giraffe today. Gorgeous! I'd never get away with eye lashes like that! Unoka's kpelle, the old men, have met and decided not to let the women vote in next month's elections, even though they have the right under Tambia's constitution. Aagh! Keep calm and carry on. Damien's dumped Stephanie? Never!? Let me sit down! Damien sees the whole world through the hole in the end of his prick. I don't know how I ever did. Vodka. Tell Stephie to get herself down the well woman clinic and have a scrape. Forget diamonds, a girl's best friend is a bent coat hanger. Sorry. I'm absolutely trolleyed.

KEITH: I've worked out why this is called The Idiot's Guide to Islam. It's written by a fucking idiot. It's politically correct, mendacious, lying crap.

LAURA: It's an approved text in Tower Hamlets.

(*Out front.*) I've just been dumped too, for what it's worth. Do you remember Lookout Masulu? He's gone back to his wives. Three of them. That's the trouble with men nowadays, they want it all.

KEITH: (*Reading.*) What! 'Jabir Ibn Haiyan is considered to be the father of modern chemistry!' Bollocks!

LAURA: You're funny when you're angry.

KEITH: They're claiming trigonometry, astronomy, mathematics. Ha! What were the Greeks doing a thousand years earlier? I suppose Archimedes was running a tourist moped franchise?!

LAURA: Don't bend it!

KEITH: A Muslim did not invent algebra! They conquered the Byzantine empire by war –

LAURA: – I know that.

KEITH: They nicked all the learning of the Greeks and translated it into Arabic! Since when has nicking been inventing?!

LAURA: Can I have my book back please!!!

KEITH: Burn it!

LAURA giggles. Enter MONDAY.

Just come in. Don't knock.

MONDAY: I have spoken with the earth spirit.

KEITH: Oh fuck.

MONDAY: Many days and many nights, and many pots of palm wine. He is angry that I do not have a bride. He say's a person's character is what he or she does when the lights go out. I have promised to apply myself to my labours in order to raise a bride price. I will sell twice as much water! All the money will go into a pot with a narrow top, so I can't get my hand in. Also, better late than never, I will stop drinking. I am no longer going to be a Christian of an evening!

He crushes the hat and throws it away.

LAURA: Monday, the…er…whilst you've been away, er…there's like a –

KEITH: – There's a standpost in the village now.

LAURA: A tap.

MONDAY: But who will buy my water? Now I will never raise a bride price.

MONDAY picks up the drinking hat, dusts it down, and puts it on.

Don't wait up!

He walks off stage left.

KEITH: Wupsadaisy!

LAURA: Did you get your post?

KEITH: Denise.

LAURA: Is whatshisname still getting bullied? Mathew, Mark, Luke –

KEITH: Jacob. He's got sticky out ears. They call him 'wingnut'. She wants the money for a private operation. I'll give her the money and next time I go home, he won't have had his ears done, and I won't get me money back.

LAURA: This is the woman you're gonna marry. I was 'Screw' at school. Laura Bolt. Bolt / Screw. That's girls for you. Sex that's all we think about. You've got seven kids by Denise?

KEITH: Yeah.

LAURA: Have you never heard of condoms?

KEITH: They're not all mine.

LAURA: Whoever's fucking your wife should be wearing condoms then.

KEITH: You're drunk.

LAURA: Yeah. Why aren't you drunk?

KEITH: You've got very crude recently.

LAURA: Fucking Ibrahima, is that charity? Is that aid work?

KEITH: You don't know the first thing about that.

LAURA: I thought the hoovering had a kinda manic, itchy edge to it, know what I mean. When do you and Ibrahima do it?

KEITH: How much have you had to drink?

LAURA: Do you wait for me to go on my rounds?

KEITH: You should find someone to fuck.

LAURA: My dad's favourite word. Should.

KEITH: When I was in Bangla Desh in 95 I organised a three-day seminar to discuss the whole concept of sex and the NGO worker. Difficult for you girls, you can't fuck the locals or you become a whore, but you know, most of you are in your twenties and –

LAURA: – up for it.

KEITH: Yeah.

LAURA: What did the 'three-day seminar' conclude?

KEITH: There were no conclusive conclusions. Truth is, for casual sex, your choice is pretty much restricted to your colleagues.

LAURA: Are you offering?

KEITH: In this job, you have to stop being idealistic and become a pragmatist.

LAURA: You're so romantic. What's it like with Ibrahima? A circumcised woman? Can she enjoy sex?

KEITH: I thought girls talked.

LAURA: What's she had, a little nick, or the full pharonic clitoridectomy with flaps off.

KEITH: Oh bloody hell.

LAURA: Why's it called pharonic? Is that after the Egyptian Pharos? It's can't be named after the Faroe Islands – Puaa! (*Spits out drink.*)

During the next they've both got the giggles.

KEITH: There's Irish medics working on the delta to try and … what's the fucking word?

LAURA: (*Through hysterical giggles.*) Stop?

KEITH: That's it. Stop it. Shh! Listen! They call a pharonic a 'short back and sides'.

They laugh. And then KEITH tops up the drinks. LAURA recovers.

LAURA: Oh God. Na zdravie!

KEITH: Cheers!

LAURA: How many women have you had, you know, in your life. Ten, twenty?

KEITH: I've been doing this job twenty years.

LAURA: Fifty, sixty?

KEITH: Three hundred.

LAURA: Three fucking hundred?! Ha, ha! Do you like sex?

KEITH: Yes.

LAURA: Do you like women?

KEITH: Yes.

LAURA: Yeah?

KEITH: Yes.

LAURA: You left your wives.

KEITH: Yeah, but fucking hell. What about you? How many blokes?

LAURA: Fourteen.

KEITH: Not bad going.

LAURA: What's the weirdest place you've ever had sex?

KEITH: Hull.

They laugh.

LAURA: I mean, like, in a combined harvester or at the dentists, or –

KEITH: – what about you?

LAURA: Me? In a tree.

KEITH: A tree?!

LAURA: Yeah. It wasn't easy. Oh, fuck. I was... Alan... there was a big power station and a ...

(*Basically gone, but still talking.*)... duck..one of them mallards...I was... I need an umbrella...no, he's not....Tuesdays and Thursdays ...

LAURA slips into unconsciousness. LAURA slides off her chair, and goes into a drunken sleep on the floor.

KEITH: I think I've got this one.

(*Out front.*) The vestry of Winchester Cathedral. I'm twennie two. Black bikers' jacket, 'White Riot' in white paint. Frown. Winter. A challenge to God. If you exist, fucking show yourself. Mel Katz, American at LSE. She's wearing a leopardskin top and leather jeans. She's a rich girl, but the Clash City Rocker forgives her, why? Cos she's gorgeous, stupid. We've planned it. I am brave until I actually get there. She pulls me into the cathedral. Inside, she rubs my cock through my jeans. I see her staring people out. She undoes the buttons on her leopardskin shirt, her nipples are hard, people stare, 'do you wanna photograph?!'. She leans back on the font. I say 'I can't, I can't, not here'. A tour party flood in from the vestry, we walk past them. The vestry is ours, she laughs, lies on the stone floor, I stand over her, look around, I can't do it, she lifts her bum off the stone, slides her jeans and knickers down. I have to help, I kneel and pull them down to her ankles. A challenge to God. If you exist show yourself now. This one's for the nuns. She opens her shirt completely and lets her head lie back. I get hard. I put a condom on. I check it, I squeeze the air out of the end. I kneel over her, and enter her. She laughs, and pulls me on, 'fuck me, come on, fuck me.' I come. The condom is split, ragged. I look up, there are three windows, The Father, The Son, and the The Holy Ghost. The sun is shining, and a ray of light twinkles through Christ's eyes. We go for the abortion together, in Birmingham, a private clinic, I borrow a car from a friend, it starts to rain, and then it stops raining, the water on the M1 turns to liquid dirt, a lorry passes, sprays us, the screen wash doesn't work, the wipers paint the screen brown like a roller spreading emulsion. A challenge to God. If you exist, show yourself now. In the ambulance I'm still conscious, 'she'll be alright son, they'll cut her out, just lie back'. I don't go to New York for the funeral. I go to Heathrow. I sit and log her flight as it climbs to the top of the departures screen. When it goes off the screen, I stand up and go to the pre-flight prayer area. The Holy Trinity window there is not real. The plaque describes it as a representation of the window in the vestry of Winchester Cathedral. Someone behind me opens a door and light floods in, and Christ's eyes twinkle.

Silence.

KEITH finishes his drink. He then stands and checks that LAURA has not swallowed her tongue, and just moves her head slightly so she can breathe. He gently moves a lock of hair from her face. He studies whatever exposed flesh there is, then gently picks at her T shirt to reveal some midriff, confident of her lack of consciousness. He then picks her up and carries her into the ibi turning left into his room. We see him place her on his bed and then he closes the shutters.

To black.

INTERVAL

September

MONDAY: (*Out front.*) Wale Adenuga, my father's father's grandfather, was not a warrior, he was a story teller, and the first man in Unoka to see an iron cow. He told this story every week of his life and he was still telling it on the day they carried him back into the forest to sleep the long sleep. He was weeding his land when he heard a strange thunder. He called the Poro and they came with their machetes. A white man came out of the forest riding on a great iron cow. The white man could not even speak properly and had a Kebbe man with him to change his words. 'There is only one God' said the white man, 'and he gave us a son, Jesus Christ, who is also a god, a god who is both man and God, and then there is the Holy Ghost. You must not worship false gods, and it is wrong to eat human flesh'. The Poro warriors wanted to kill the white man but Wale Adenuga knew that he could destroy the white man with words. 'You say there is only *one* God. And this One God has a son called Jesus, who is also a god. Things must be different where you come from, because here, in Unoka, one and one makes two.' The Poro had never laughed so loud. The white man turned red, and they had never seen skin change colour, so they laughed even harder, and Wale Adenuga with skill was riding the laughter like a snake on the white water. 'And this brother of the One and only God, the quiet one, the Holy Ghost, he must be a god too, so that's three gods, and the big One God if he has a son, must have a wife, who would have to be a god too, because the big One God would not want to lay down with the daughter of a yam farmer. So that is four gods already, but wait, I need a piss!' And Wale Adenuga walked over to the iron cow and pissed against the wheels, and as he pissed he carried on counting, 'four, five, six gods, seven' and all the Poro laughed, and no work at all was done that day in the fields, and the women were brought together and Wale Adenuga was made to tell the story again and again, until he fell down drunk from palm wine and happiness.

(*Beat.*) Three market weeks later the white man returned with warriors wearing coats made of blood. They went into the bush to where the young Poro where living, and learning the ways of the forest. Twenty-three boys were killed. The Poro collected their bodies and ate their hearts so that their power was not wasted and today their spirits live on, and they are forever with the Kebbe.

KEITH and LAURA sit. KEITH is reading a letter. IBRAHIMA is seen in the background, cleaning. A television and satellite dish, both still boxed, are set by the gate to the road.

LAURA: (*Out front.*) Dear Pip. You are not a lesbian. Everybody fancies Björk. I do, and so does my mother. You've read the Koran in two days! Yeah, it is, as you say, a beautiful text, and stylistically much more interesting than the bible. And yes, of course, Britain has become an entirely alcoholic nation. Very astute of you, oh vodka queen. Yes, I agree, Muslims are so right, acts of violence are almost always caused by alcohol. Except maybe the Iran Iraq war. One million Muslims dead and not a babycham between them.

(*To KEITH.*) Have you seen the newsletter.

KEITH: (*Engrossed in his own letter.*) Yeah. Terrible, innit.

LAURA: They, like, executed them! I mean, why?

KEITH: They're Brits. Brits / Americans. Iraq? (*Laughing.*) Ha, ha! Pauline has become a Buddhist. The butcher's kicked her out. Said she was beginning to undermine his confidence. She's changed her name to Hari.

LAURA: Harry?

KEITH: No. H.A.R.I.

LAURA: Does that mean anything?

KEITH: Gullible white girl.

LAURA: No.

KEITH: Is Yahiya expecting me?

LAURA: Yeah, but ring, check.

KEITH dials from his mobile.

I went to see the Dalai Lama when I was in Rio. He was supporting Sting. What have you got against Buddhists?

KEITH: None of them can cook, yet they all insist on running fucking cafes. Thai Buddhists are alright. They eat meat. When I was working with the prostitutes in Pat Pong –

LAURA: – Where?

KEITH: Bangkok, Thailand. Ha! That was a good gig.

(*On the phone.*) Yahiya? It's me……here, she won't talk to me.

He passes over the phone.

LAURA: Eeeeee! Agi, agi! ……Mr. Keith he will bring the television today…thirteen inch…no we don't have Hitachis……Have you got your money through?…. Good….Agi, agi!

Phone off.

KEITH: They fucking love you don't they?

LAURA: Do you think we've gone too far?

KEITH: One television in every village is hardly a revolution is it.

LAURA: Two televisions in every village. One for the girls and one for the boys.

KEITH: Course.

LAURA: What do the boys watch?

KEITH: Al Jazeera, Turkish porn and golf.

LAURA: The girls watch Al Jazeera and Turkish porn.
They don't like golf.

KEITH: The internet next. I must write to Bill Gates. Email.

Enter MONDAY. He gives KEITH a piece of paper.

Where's my fucking drill?

MONDAY and KEITH face off for a moment.

What's this?

MONDAY: My joinery homework.

LAURA: I think this joiner thing is a cool idea. You'll raise
a bride price –

MONDAY: – If you had not brought a tap to the village I
would have a big fat wife already!

LAURA: Monday, can you go with Keith in the puk puk
and take a television up to Yahiya in Maduka?

MONDAY: No! Tuesday is my wild movie night!

LAURA: Pornography.

MONDAY: You can call it pornography but sometimes
there is a good story and interesting characters, but not
often, thank God! You know, there is something
wonderful about sitting around in a darkened room with
fifteen Kebbe brothers all with a big bamboo.

KEITH: How many tons of maize will this design hold?

MONDAY: It's a CD rack.

KEITH: I asked you to design a maize crib.

MONDAY: I don't need a maize crib! I've got two CDs and nowhere to put them!

LAURA: What are your CDs?

MONDAY: 2pac, 'fucking with the wrong nigga', and Charlotte Church. Charlotte Church is my favourite. The voice of a virgin! And the body of a virgin, let's hope! If not, we've all been done!

LAURA: The maize cribs round here –

MONDAY: – our maize cribs have been like that since Muhammad.

KEITH: The cobs on the bottom always rot!

MONDAY: That's how it works! The bottom cobs rot, so the top ones don't.

KEITH: No cobs have to rot!

MONDAY: Your head has become a coconut.

LAURA: You'll raise a bride price quicker this way.

MONDAY: Soon I will have three wives and much cooking on the go.

KEITH: What are you up to? Where's my drill?

MONDAY: I am now in the oil business.

KEITH: Stealing diesel.

MONDAY: I am Kebbe. It is Kebbe diesel.

KEITH: Your government sold the oil.

MONDAY: My government are not Kebbe.

KEITH: Fucked!

LAURA: How much do you get for a can of diesel?

MONDAY: Every day is different. Today, many hungry lions.

LAURA: It's incredibly dangerous drilling into the pipe, you know, in Nigeria –

MONDAY: – Nigerians were not behind the door when brains were given out!

KEITH: The drill?

MONDAY: I will give you money.

MONDAY gets a significant wad of money out.

KEITH: I don't want money, I want my fucking drill. Do you know what the curse of the thief is?

MONDAY: Success!

KEITH: I taught you that.

MONDAY: (*Angry.*) You have always tried to teach me many things when all I ever needed was a bloody drill!

KEITH: I'm going. I'm gonna take the puk puk.

KEITH leaves taking the boxed television with him.

LAURA: You know this maize cribs thing. I think that's a good idea.

MONDAY: I am not a bloody farmer!

LAURA: I remember when you wanted to be a farmer, you said it was a man's job. It's this new Imam isn't it?

MONDAY: He fainted today when we killed the sheep! He is very sophisticated, very city. Shit and him have never met!

LAURA: What does he have to say about the destruction of the twin towers?

MONDAY: What? Wembley?

LAURA: The World Trade Centre.

MONDAY: He is selling the video.

LAURA: Oh no!

MONDAY: There is two hours of Ali Bakassa talking at the beginning but you can fast forward through that bit.

LAURA: And these videos are being played on our TVs?

MONDAY: The top seller! Would you like one?

LAURA: I feel a bit sick.

MONDAY: Today, he has given us all the nod to beat our wives! But I am sad, I do not have a wife.

LAURA: (*Angry.*) And, like, exactly why are the wives going to be beaten?

MONDAY: 'For the things they might have done!'

LAURA: That is pathetic!

MONDAY: It is very wise. Before the tap arrived the women spent five hours a day collecting water, but now, for them each day is a pick and mix of temptations. They might be drinking; might be fornicating; might be thinking about drinking and fornicating; they might be voting in the elections, then having one for the road, and then back for more fornication! So tonight we men are doing Allah's work and guarding the polling stations here in Unoka and up in Enuga.

LAURA: Why Enuga?

MONDAY: When the polling station closes we can go straight to the wild movie club.

LAURA: I know I've only read the Idiot's Guide but obviously there is absolutely no endorsement for this kind of violence towards women in the Koran.

MONDAY: Ali Bakassa reads the Koran several times every day. And he has found it by diligent study.

LAURA: 'It'?

MONDAY opens his copy of the Koran at a marked page.

MONDAY: (*Reading.*) 'As to those women from whom you fear defiant sinfulness' – (*Translating.*) – if you 'think' your wife *might* be sinful –

(*Reading.*) 'first admonish them, then refuse to share your bed with them'

(*Translating.*) – tick her off, if that doesn't work spend all night on the settee in a big fuck off sulk –

(*Reading.*) 'and then, if necessary, slap them.'

LAURA: Hit her?

MONDAY: Yes! With a toothbrush!

LAURA: Hit her with a toothbrush?

MONDAY: Oh yes! A man once asked Muhammad, peace be upon him, for advice on the best way to beat his wife and Muhammad, peace be upon him, happened to be brushing his teeth at the time, and so Muhammad, peace be upon him, said 'hit her with a toothbrush'. But Ali Bakassa he says that the toothbrush is a metaphor!

LAURA: For what?

MONDAY: A very big stick!

LAURA: Look, don't you think it's more likely that Muhammad –

MONDAY: – Peace be upon him!

LAURA: – meant, kinda, don't beat your wife at all when he said a toothbrush because, you know, it's not easy to hurt someone with a toothbrush.

MONDAY: You have only read some crappy paperback written by an American girl. I will take your motorbike.

Exit MONDAY. LAURA sits. A mobile phone goes off. She thinks it's hers and picks it out of her pocket only to discover that it is not hers. Enter IBRAHIMA on the phone.

IBRAHIMA: (*On the phone.*) Yeeee! Chim kolle fum age fum. Eeee! Agi, agi! Swayinka! Fem, fem, agi, agi! Bloody silly ring tone! Chem sway! Enuga. Yee! Agi, agi. Enuga! Ciao.

LAURA: (*Happy.*) You're so big now?

IBRAHIMA: (*Not happy.*) Yes.

LAURA: What's wrong?

IBRAHIMA: If the child is another 'not a boy' my husband will kill me.

LAURA: No, no, I don't think….will he?

IBRAHIMA: He said even a poor man can have too many sticks.

LAURA: When is it due?

IBRAHIMA: The last market week in December. I have to go to the mountain a month before it is due.

LAURA: That's, like, Sande stuff, yeah?

IBRAHIMA: Yes. The Earth Spirit will decide whether it is to be a boy.

LAURA: But your six months already, the sex is already…. no.

IBRAHIMA: What?

LAURA: Nothing.

IBRAHIMA: (*Conspiratorial.*) I am going to vote tonight.

LAURA: But the kpelle had a meeting, they agreed that the women would not be allowed to vote.

IBRAHIMA: Fuck the kpelle! We women have the right to vote! Tambia is a very modern democracy. Tambia will be sending representatives to monitor the fairness of the next American elections. That's my little joke.

LAURA: That's a very good little joke. But I don't want you to vote. It's dangerous, there are –

IBRAHIMA: – the President of Bangla Desh is a woman, and so is the Deputy Prime Minister of Iran, and then there's Imran Khan's wife.

LAURA: What's she?

IBRAHIMA: A woman. We cannot vote here in Unoka because the diesel boys are guarding the polling station, so we will walk over the hills to Enuga.

LAURA: Don't try and vote O.K.! I don't want you to vote. Have you got that? At no point did I ever suggest that you should exercise your democratic right to vote. O.K.?

IBRAHIMA: (*genuinely angry.*) Voting is my idea!

LAURA: Oh God, you don't understand, these things are like subtle, I mean – alright! Do what you like, but it has nothing to do with me.

IBRAHIMA moves towards the gate.

Don't go to Enuga.

IBRAHIMA: What?

LAURA: There will be men there. Monday has gone up there with the Imam and a gang from the mosque.

IBRAHIMA: Today is the last chance to vote.

LAURA and IBRAHIMA both get on their mobile phones and make calls. LAURA's voice dominates.

LAURA: (*On the phone.*) Keith?… it's me… Where are you?…can you see the polling station?….are there any men stopping the women voting….O.K. cool, see you later.

(*Off the phone.*) Maduka.

IBRAHIMA: Maduka, in the barn?

LAURA: Yes.

IBRAHIMA: (*On the phone.*) Yee! It's me…. Agi, Maduka…. Yes, there are men at Enuga. You ring Mgbafo, I will ring Kiaga. Get Mgbafo to ring Odema and pass it on. Agi!

IBRAHIMA leaves with a wave, still on the phone.

LAURA: Oh fuck!

To black and end of scene.

October

IBRAHIMA stands with her face upstage. LAURA stands upstage of her. Slowly she lifts the burqa over her head. Her head is completely bandaged. LAURA carefully places the burqa over her face, she goes into the ibi to work.

To black.

A lap top is set up and in use by KEITH. LAURA is downstage holding her post which is a large A4+ sized envelope which has been opened roughly and resealed using a Tambian Customs seal.

LAURA: (*Out front.*) Dear Pip. I know you sent me a copy of *Heat* but customs must have nicked it! Aagh! I believe you because there's a Toni and Guy voucher in the envelope. My girls tried to vote last month, but they were attacked by the Diesel Boys. When Ibrahima's husband heard he threw kerosene on her, and set light to her. She's lost her hair, and the flesh on her ears. Keith and I went to the police. Joke! Do you remember the night of the tap celebrations? I got totally lashed. Well, I woke up in Keith's bed. He was in the chair. He said he wanted to make sure I didn't do a Jimi Hendrix so he put me on the bed face down. I don't think he did anything but, I don't know. I should have told you last month. You feel a long way away Pip.

(*To MONDAY, angry.*) Did any women try and vote in Enuga?

MONDAY: I've told you!

KEITH: Oi!

MONDAY: I didn't hit anyone!

KEITH: Cool it! Let's have a drink.

MONDAY: All the hitting was at Maduka!

KEITH: (*To MONDAY.*) We're out of vodka.

LAURA: Muslim heaven's not short of booze is it.

KEITH: Let it lie!

MONDAY: Oh yes, Muslim heaven is very good! We are all just warming up for one big jam session!

LAURA: Yeah!

KEITH: (*Singing.*) 'Everyone is trying to get to the bar – '

LAURA: – you can't sing!

KEITH: '– name of the bar, the bar is called heaven.' Talking Heads. 'Fear of Music'. Good album. Interesting use of minor keys. Too esoteric of course to be an important band.

LAURA: Muslim heaven is just Booze and girls isn't it!?

MONDAY: There will also be many beautiful fountains.

LAURA: I bet there's a fuck of a queue for the fountains.

KEITH: I'm the boss here, right? I said –

LAURA: (*To KEITH.*) – No! I'm fucked off.

(*To MONDAY.*) These whatsaname sex slaves –

MONDAY: The houris. Built for sex!

LAURA: Lara Crofts. They don't have souls, they're not real women, not human.

KEITH: Course they're not human, it's heaven.

LAURA: But no souls!

MONDAY: Brilliant! No bloody waterworks when you dump them!?

KEITH: What do you know about dumping women?

MONDAY: I listen to the world service! Also, in Muslim heaven everyone is about thirty.

LAURA: Sounds like Crouch End.

KEITH: (*To MONDAY.*) You might go to hell. You're a thief, a wanker, a Christian, an alcoholic, you worship Poro gods.

MONDAY: – Muslim hell is much better too, it's temporary! Christian hell is forever! Very bad!

LAURA: What's Muslim hell like then?

MONDAY: Fountains of pus, blood, and boiling muck, and utter hopelessness and despair everywhere.

KEITH/LAURA: Crouch End.

LAURA: (*In his face.*) Muslim heaven seems to me like a pornographic fantasy. One long, immature, teenage boy's wank.

MONDAY exits.

KEITH: Monday!

(*To LAURA.*) Brilliant.

LAURA: I'm sorry. Where will he go?

KEITH: On the piss.

KEITH picks up MONDAY's blue fez Christian clan hat.

LAURA: He's forgotten his drinking hat. Oh shit!

She grabs the hat and rushes into the road.

KEITH: Oh wupsadaisy!

LAURA: He's gone. Fuck!

KEITH: He'll be alright. Do you wanna spliff? Don't let the bastards grind you down.

KEITH lights a spliff.

LAURA: What are you grinning at?

KEITH: Listening to a feminist having a go at Islam is about all the fun I can handle.

LAURA: I'm not a bloody feminist! How can I be? I'm only twenty-four.

KEITH: (*Laughs.*) Feminism eh? The dog that didn't bark.

LAURA: What?

KEITH: (*Chuckling.*) They've left Islam well alone haven't they. Daren't start, cos it'd make their little western whinges look very silly. Wages for house work. Huh. Glass ceilings, huh, huh!

LAURA: Listen. Ibrahima's baby is due next month. If it's another 'not a boy' he'll kill her.

KEITH: He might not.

LAURA: He fucking will! And what are we going to do about it?

KEITH: We can't get involved.

LAURA: We are involved. You've been using her for sex, we're –

KEITH: Prostitution is consenting sex. Between adults.

LAURA: Why don't you get yourself a Philippino catalogue bride, settle down in Oldham and stop inflicting yourself on the third world, you wanker?!

KEITH: I wish you wouldn't use the term 'the third world'.

LAURA: If she has a girl and he kills her. I think I'll fucking kill him. I'll buy a Kalashnikov from Monday. I will!

KEITH: Has she been to the mountain yet?

LAURA: No. She goes quite soon.

KEITH: Wait for that then.

LAURA: What? You're not serious. You're as bad as they are. It's either a boy or a girl already.

KEITH: Faith.

LAURA: Fuck faith.

KEITH: Shh!

Enter IBRAHIMA.

IBRAHIMA: Hi.

LAURA: Hi.

KEITH: Hi.

IBRAHIMA: Do you have the internet working?

KEITH: Not yet. Almost. I've set you up an account. ibrahima dot globeact @ aol.com. I'll write it down for you.

IBRAHIMA: My own email! Eeéeee! Agi! Are you still leaving after Christmas?

KEITH: Laura is taking over.

IBRAHIMA: But the computer will stay?

KEITH: Yes.

IBRAHIMA: I would like to run this place.

KEITH: Your husband will want you to look after the boy.

IBRAHIMA: Yes.

KEITH: Laura will talk to all the women and see what can be done.

LAURA: Where will you give birth?

IBRAHIMA: In my ibi. With the other wives and my sisters.

LAURA: I will pay for you to go to Kante, the hospital
    there –

KEITH: Laura!

LAURA: – has got good facilities and I'll stay with you
    and –

KEITH: You can't save these people from themselves.

LAURA: (*With sarcasm.*) It's like herding cats.

KEITH: There is only one hope.

LAURA: A Christian God? You know, for someone like me,
    I mean, there was a time when I would have wanted
    there to be a God, it woulda been kinda nice, you know,
    but not now cos the really really stupid thing about, you
    know, the world now, yeah, is that there is no God, he or
    she is dead, in fact never was. So the whole premise of
    religion is a complete fucking fantasy non-starter, and
    the little history thing between Christianity or the West
    and Islam is utterly pathetic because it's the same God of
    course, the same God that doesn't exist. But if you say
    these gobsmackinglyobvious things it makes it worse
    doesn't it. If you tell people like you to pack up and go
    home, or tell the Imam to fuck off back to Medina, they
    come out spitting fire, cos you've taken away the only
    idea they've got, and you're asking them to face up to
    the difficult and dispiriting job of living, here, now, on
    earth, with each other. And all they're left with these
    people, you!, is people, and people like you hate people
    because people are sinners.

    (*Beat.*) Don't take notes, there's a handout at the end.

    (*To IBRAHIMA.*) Sorry about this.

KEITH: Only –

LAURA: – I haven't finished! I'm the really brave one here, because I've made the tough decision not to, like, console myself with a fucking fairy tale, a ready-made answer to the question that, like, has no answer and will never have a fucking answer. Who are we? And, like, why are we here? I mean it's like as if the whole world is made up of five-year-olds who believe in Father Christmas. It is not a sensible way to run a fucking planet!!

KEITH: I pity you.

Internet connection noises.

Here we go!

(*Beat.*) I'm through! Come on, come on.

The AOL voice sounds. 'YOU HAVE EMAIL'.

Yes! Ha, ha!

LAURA: What is it?

KEITH: Yup. Chuck and Patti from Care in Kante.

(*Reading.*) They're in Kante for a 'thanksgiving' lunch but would love to come to the beautiful Unoka for a turkey lunch on Christmas day.

LAURA: Where are you getting a turkey? No-one round here farms turkeys.

KEITH: I'm getting it Fedexed. Ibrahima's got mail! Ha, ha!

LAURA: You're having a turkey posted here?

KEITH: Yeah, from Oldham. I've done it before. Ibrahima!

LAURA: It takes two weeks, if you're lucky.

KEITH: Me mother cooks it, freezes it and vacuum seals it. Puts it in a cool box and labels it Essential Medical supplies and it takes a week.

(*To IBRAHIMA.*) You've got mail.

IBRAHIMA: Email? Me? EEEEeeeee! Agi! Agi!!

KEITH: Yeah.

IBRAHIMA: (*To LAURA.*) 'I've got mail!'

LAURA: Yes.

KEITH: Just double click.

LAURA: Who's it from?

IBRAHIMA: (*Reading.*) 'Expand, lengthen and enlarge the girth of your penis.'

To black.

November

MONDAY is being flogged.

MONDAY: (*Out front.*) I am a Christian!

(*Lash.*) Agh!

(*Lash.*) Agh! I was drinking but I have a Christian name.

(*Lash.*) Agh! Monday! My name is Monday. An old English name!

(*Lash.*) Agh! You cannot lash an Englishman!

(*Lash.*) Agh! I am not in the mosque. My father is the mission.

(*Lash.*) Agh! Your law is not my law!

(*Lash.*) Agh! Do I have a beard!? I lost my hat on the road!

(*Lash.*) Agh! I am Egwome Christian, Kante Egwome. My hat –

(*Lash.*) Agh. (*Laughing.*) I lost my hat in the wind.

(*Lash.*) (*Laughing.*) The wind blew my hat off!

(*Lash.*)

(*Lash.*)

(*Lash.*)

(*Lash.*) I am Poro. I am Kebbe.

To black. Lights up on IBRAHIMA and LAURA.

IBRAHIMA is very pregnant. LAURA is hugging her, and crying.

LAURA: I wish I could come with you. Ask the Earth Spirit for a boy, from me.

IBRAHIMA: It is not good to ask too hard. Where's Keith?

LAURA: He went to see that Monday was lashed properly, you know, humanely. Is there anything I can do?

IBRAHIMA: Are you are a Christian?

LAURA: Yes. I am a Christian.

IBRAHIMA: Pray to your God then.

IBRAHIMA kisses LAURA and walks off stage left.

LAURA: (*Out front.*) Pip 27 @ hotmail.com Subject. A prayer for Ibrahima. I am so ashamed that we are on AOL. Uuugh! We're a bloody NGO for Christ's sake! NGO not VSO, O.K.? You want my advice? O.K. Here goes. I know you're in deep shit with Uni debts and credit cards and I know you're, like, totally deconstructed over Barry, still, but I am absolutely solid that going to America to sell your eggs is wrong. Ethically and morally, and you won't make that much money anyway, not after all your costs. Now I need a favour. Remember that internet chain letter you organised for the Mujahidin human rights at Guantanamo Bay. Well, basically I want a global chain prayer thingy for a woman called Ibrahima in Unoka, Tambia. She is due to give birth and if the child is a girl, her husband will kill her. He will. Please Pip. Kiss, kiss, kiss.

To black.

Enter MONDAY wearing shorts and flip flops only. He is carrying an AK47 which he gives to LAURA.

LAURA: I don't want it.

MONDAY: It is mine. Take it from me, please, and lock it in the safe. I want to use it.

LAURA takes it.

IBRAHIMA: (*Out front.*) Earth Spirit. I am Sande. You are God of All things. I have washed. I have eaten. I carry one of yours. It is time for you to decide. I am now nine months without bleeding and the child is ready. I have been here at the mountain for two market weeks. I have not looked at pictures.

She flinches slightly with guilt.

(*Less confidently.*) I have not listened to words. My little God is fed. I have three girls. Your decision will please me. Take this wine, it is fermented.

Her phone rings. She panics and turns it off. And starts to cry.

I have not listened to words. I have not looked at pictures. I am mountain. I am clean. I will sleep here now. I will take pleasure in your decision.

To black.

LAURA is dressing MONDAY's wounds.

MONDAY: – Agh! You are not allowed to touch me.

LAURA: Alright, I won't do it.

MONDAY: No. It is good. It is very good.

KEITH: Can someone tell me why there's an AK47 in our safe?

LAURA: Had you been drinking that night Monday?

MONDAY: Egg nog! It has me in its grip!

LAURA: Look, the Diesel boys are the bully boys for the Sharia Committee. But they nick diesel from the pipeline. They just wanted to warn you off, you know, off their diesel.

MONDAY: – Take the logs from your eyes! Of course! They were buying the bloody drinks! That's how they could be sure I was drinking!

KEITH: (*Laughing.*) Huh, you see, without the rule of law you're fucked. That's what Britain gave the world, and from that one idea, flows everything. Equal rights for all men, Shakespeare, cricket, the Clash. Look at the sports we invented: football, rugby, swimming –

LAURA: – swimming?

KEITH: The rules of swimming. Sports we didn't invent wind surfing, kick boxing, and the luge.

LAURA: 'Things we invented before the Nazis'. Concentration camps.

KEITH: The Spanish were the first to use concentration camps, in Cuba, eighteen ninety –

LAURA: – Slavery?

KEITH: We ended slavery!

LAURA: Who, like, started it though?

KEITH: The Portuguese! Actually that is the fucking problem, cos no-one is taught the bloody truth anymore are they, they're taught a concocted, apology for the truth by some twenty-two-year-old Australian supply teacher who puts a question mark at the end of every fucking sentence and thinks the Spanish Armada is a tapas bar in Putney.

LAURA: I've been there.

KEITH: We invented human rights.

LAURA/MONDAY: (*Laughs.*)

KEITH: The lawyer who started Amnesty International was an Englishman! He wasn't a fucking Libyan that's for sure. Libya, are chair of the UN Commission for Human Rights, you know. How the fuck did that happen?

LAURA: You're gonna tell us, aren't you?

KEITH: It's the African nations turn to chair that committee – as if it's a game of pass the fucking parcel. So they lock them in a room and tell them not to come out until they've chosen someone suitable. Ten minutes later out comes Colonel Gadaffi with the bin on his head. You know, sometimes I'm ashamed to be a liberal!

LAURA: It's like herding cats!

MONDAY and LAURA laugh.

KEITH: I'm a pacifist, naturally, but you've got to admit, the British army is the best in the world.

LAURA/MONDAY: (*Giggle.*)

KEITH: If it had been us at Srebrenica instead of a bunch of Dutch transvestites there would be six thousand Muslim men still alive today.

(*Double mouse click.*) Fuck! Chuck and Patti have pulled out of Christmas dinner. Worried about the diesel boys. Bloody Americans. Wimps.

MONDAY: Agh!

KEITH: (*Clicks and brings up another email.*) Peter fucking Nicholson's Global wank, sorry, update. Hi! Devastated by the atrocity at Belle Yella, bla, bla, tragic, bla, bla, wives and families, bla, bla... the work will continue.

LAURA: Why don't they just close it down? We pulled out of Pakistan.

KEITH: Belle Yella is where we started, and Peter fucking Nicholson has had his 'resolve strengthened'.

Enter IBRAHIMA. She stands and stares at LAURA.

IBRAHIMA: I have been sent the dream. Eeeee!

IBRAHIMA hugs LAURA.

KEITH: Good.

LAURA: Calm down, calm down. Just tell me.

IBRAHIMA: It is going to be a boy!

LAURA: It was a boy in the dream?

KEITH: Oh good.

IBRAHIMA: A beautiful, big, strong boy. I am so happy!

IBRAHIMA hugs LAURA again. MONDAY stands.

MONDAY: Ig bafoo kom illi fem chu aka?

IBRAHIMA: Cha! Phuttum Yazid!

MONDAY: Ig challa wole ka um fem chillo?

KEITH: Oi! Come on we've got a rule here. English!

IBRAHIMA: Swem fila chum fem chillo. Agi, swem fallah fallah chum fem chillo.

MONDAY: Agi?

IBRAHIMA: Chew fem chilla. Agi fem chillo.

MONDAY: Swayinka!

IBRAHIMA: Chem sway! Agi.

MONDAY: Agi, agi.

KEITH: Excuse me! (*To IBRAHIMA.*) The electricity's on!

LAURA: There's no need. You should rest.

(*To KEITH.*) Do you have cleaning?

KEITH: My room needs a bit of a hoover.

LAURA: We'll pay you just the same, can't we?

KEITH: No. Do some work. What was all that about? You two are normally like cat and dog.

MONDAY: We are both Poro.

KEITH: Come on!

MONDAY: The Earth Spirit gave her a message dream. We thought he was dead.

LAURA: But he gave you a dream in the summer about selling more water, to get a wife.

MONDAY: I made that up.

LAURA: Everybody dreams. How do you know it's, like, a proper one.

MONDAY: In the dream your little God is taken to a cave, and you can look down and see yourself.

LAURA: Where are you going?

MONDAY: The forest. The human mind is like a parachute, it works best when it is open! After that flagrant flogging I am sticking two fingers up to Ali Bakassa. The Poro is a very natural way of life. Eating is good, drinking is very good, and fornication is absolutely essential!

KEITH: And cannibalism?

MONDAY: You can call it cannibalism. We call it 'eating people'.

LAURA: Do the Poro really, like, eat, you know, actual people?

MONDAY: Only the best! You are what you eat!

KEITH: It's barbaric.

MONDAY: (*Confrontational. In KEITH's face.*) When the Kebbe first cultivated this land we made an agreement with the Earth Spirit. But the big whitey 'One God' put a stop to all the sacrifices and the important eating and what happens?! Before you can say 'Ben Jonson!' Bang! No rains! No yams! No maize! And then brother is killing brother.

KEITH: You flunked out of bush school. Why? Couldn't eat the flesh eh?

MONDAY: It was me they were going to eat! Eating is good. Being eaten is not so good. But I am going back to the forest now. He is alive.

KEITH: No you're bloody not. You work here. You're paid by us.

MONDAY: You people believe in nothing.

KEITH: I believe in the Lord God our Father who –

MONDAY: – Your father's arse is on fire!

Exit MONDAY.

To black.

December

MONDAY: Earth Spirit. I am Poro. I am Kebbe. I bring myself to you. I have not washed. I have not looked at pictures, not heard the words of the big whitey, not heard the words of the beards. My head is empty. There is space now. I am the forest. My little God is in me. He said go to the forest. I am here. I know you live. It is my little God you hear speaking. Take him from my body. Give him dreams. Accept me now – take my gifts. My little God will listen. I am empty now. You can fill me. I am the forest. Give me dreams.

A little Christmas tree with lights running off a battery with a cross on top. Christmas crackers on the table. An advent calendar, with all the windows open. On the table a fedex box marked 'medical supplies / express'.

LAURA: (*Out front.*) Pip27 @ hotmail dot com. Subject. Happy Christmas. Not. My dad has left my mum. He's met someone younger, better looking, with a more attractive personality. Also, two days ago, in Pakistan, a bus carrying Muslim girls was hijacked by Christian boys and seven of the girls were raped at gunpoint. Al Jazeera got hold of some amateur film of it and have been playing the footage over and over again. Here in Tambia, the diesel boys and other Muslim vigilante groups went bananas and attacked all the 'Death is Certain' buses and burned all the 'God is in Control' toilet paper they could find. Public Christian worship, and Christmas celebrations have been banned.

Enter KEITH from the road.

Wow! Twenty seven thousand people prayed for Ibrahima. You're incredible. Brill, thanks, Pip. She's gone into labour.

Enter KEITH from the road. LAURA stands. They face each other.

KEITH: She's had the baby. Half an hour ago.

Pause.

LAURA: Tell me then. Just fucking tell me!

KEITH: Calm down.

LAURA: No! No! I will not fucking calm down! Tell me!

KEITH: It's a boy! A boy!

LAURA does a mixture of laughter and tears and drops to her knees.

LAURA: (*Through laughter and tears.*) I don't believe it. I can't believe it. A boy. A boy! Oh God!

KEITH: She's alright. They're both alright.

LAURA: (*Through tears.*) I don't believe it. I just knew, I absolutely solidly knew that it was going to be a girl. I was beginning to feel as if someone kinda had it in for me, and every terrible thing that has ever happened in the world was being put before me, to kinda, you know, I dunno, test me. A boy! But this is good. This is very, very good.

She starts to cry. KEITH puts his arms around her. She freezes. She tries to push him off.

No!

KEITH: I'm sorry?

LAURA: Just don't fucking touch me.

KEITH: Woah!

LAURA: Yeah.

KEITH: What's going on?

LAURA: That night, you know, when we got drunk, the tap celebration night.

KEITH: Yeah.

LAURA: You looked after me. You put me in your bed, and you slept in the chair.

KEITH: Yeah.

LAURA: Did you do anything? To me.

KEITH: I put you in bed, I made sure you were face down –

LAURA: – so I didn't choke on my vomit. Did you do anything else?

KEITH: I see. No. After I *looked after you*, I went to sleep.

LAURA: Why did Victoria go home?

KEITH: She's was a nutter. She had a severe reaction to the malaria tablets, she was hallucinating for a whole week. I took her to the hospital. They had to strap her to the fucking bed. She thought she was a monkey. She was going to scale the outside of the building.

LAURA: I don't believe you.

KEITH: Why should I lie?

LAURA: You've lied before. She never got drunk at the army barracks. She never gave anyone a blow job in public.

KEITH: Yeah, I made that up. I was trying to make a point for your benefit. I didn't touch you.

LAURA: Did you spike my drink? O.K. How about this? I think you spiked my drink, and then, I dunno, played with me, fingered me, fucked me.

KEITH: (*Angry.*) I stopped you choking on your own puke, put you in my bed, and went to sleep in the chair!

LAURA: Why didn't you put me in my bed?

KEITH: You don't have a chair in your room.

LAURA: Did you look at me? Did you wank?

Silence.

(*As a statement.*) You had a wank.

Pause.

KEITH: I didn't touch you. I didn't harm you at all.

LAURA: See you later.

LAURA makes to leave.

KEITH: You're beautiful. And clever. You're not going to be interested in me. Look at me. I'm a bit of a twat. But I didn't touch you.

LAURA: You thought about it, considered it.

KEITH: I'm leaving tomorrow. I just want to say, it's been great. You're great.

LAURA: I saw your tickets. You're not going home.

KEITH: No.

LAURA: Freetown. We haven't got a project in Sierra Leone.

KEITH: I go overland from Freetown. Across the Liberian border.

LAURA: Belle Yella.

KEITH: Yup. Peter fucking Nicholson wants a leapfrog technology project on the Tambian model, your model.

LAURA: Go home!

KEITH: I didn't touch you. I didn't do anything.

(*Beat.*) Do you like Yorkshire puddings?

LAURA: Yeah.

KEITH: (*Indicating the Fedex box.*) I guess this is the turkey.

KEITH starts to open the box.

LAURA: I'm going to see Ibrahima.

KEITH: Wear a burqa. A veil's not gonna be enough. Not today.

LAURA goes into the ibi. KEITH starts to open the box. He takes out the turkey. Enter LAURA dressed in a light coloured burqa.

No guns?

LAURA: No guns.

She exits stage right. KEITH picks out the turkey. It is crawling with maggots. Enter MONDAY dressed in traditional African Poro bush school dress. He is holding a machete in one hand a beard in the other. He is wearing a mask and is painted with white clay like a warrior.

KEITH: Where the fuck have you been? It's Christmas dinner, not fancy dress. I'm not paying you for the last two weeks. You're taking the piss.

The sound of motorbikes in the background. The noise level increases during the next.

Well? Cat got your tongue?

MONDAY: I have been given a dream.

KEITH: Let me guess. You were naked in the park baking bread, your mother, dressed like a schoolgirl comes in on a horse –

MONDAY: – In the dream I eat the beard of Ali Bakassa!

KEITH: Got a sense of humour then has he, the Earth Spirit. Why do you have to eat his beard?

MONDAY: The power of an imam is always in the beard.

KEITH: Course. And this is Ali Bakassa's beard?

MONDAY: I cut the hair from his chin myself!

KEITH: What with a machete?

MONDAY: (*Producing scissors.*) No I took some scissors along.

KEITH: Did anyone see you?

MONDAY: I am wearing the devil mask.

KEITH: Well that's alright then. How are you gonna eat it?

MONDAY bites off a bit of beard and starts to chew.

You'll get a hair ball.

MONDAY: I will make a sauce.

KEITH: She's had the baby. It's a boy.

MONDAY: Of course! She was given a boy in the dream.

The noise of motorbikes is heard outside.

No-one saw you eh?

KEITH peeks through holes in the fence.

The diesel boys.

MONDAY turns the Christmas tree lights off, and snatches the cross off the top and lobs it into the ibi. He goes to the gate and secures it shut. He goes into the ibi and comes out with the drill and undoes a panel in the fence. He has left the machete on the table. MONDAY rushes into the ibi and comes out with the drill. KEITH goes into the ibi and comes out with the kalashnikov.

MONDAY: Come on! Are you crazy?!

(*Beat.*) Chum kolla kwafe ma. (God help you.)

MONDAY exits through the fence. KEITH turns the Christmas lights on. He stands and stares at the door, quite calm. The door breaks open.

To black.

May

A bright sunny day. Spring. LAURA is typing away at the lap top. She has a beer open and is smoking.

LAURA: (*Out front.*) Pip27 @ hotmail.com. We've applied for a position in Bhutan. That's the eastern Himalayas. Bhutan is probably the world's most beautiful, unspoilt country. They're mainly Buddhists. The project is to try and stop nicotine and alcohol abuse spreading from the capital Thimbu into the regions. I must be mad. I love it.

Enter HARSHA. She is a young twenty-three-ish British woman, second or third generation Indian. She is dressed in jeans, a T shirt with a NO LOGO logo, (or whatever the current vogue is amongst globalisation protesters) and an improvised hijab. She carries hand luggage and a big holdall. Hanging out of the holdall is a copy of Heat *magazine. She puts her bags down.*

HARSHA: Hi. Harsha. You must be Laura.

LAURA: Hi. You're late.

HARSHA: Yeah, a couple of UN blue helmets, like, stopped the bus and took a gang off at gun point? Hey, there's a war on. Scary.

LAURA: You weren't scared at the time, but you are now?

HARSHA: Yeah! That's it.

LAURA: Do you wanna beer?

HARSHA: We've got beer? I thought this –

LAURA: – would you prefer vodka?

HARSHA: Beer's cool. I got totally wankered last night. I promised myself I'd, like, detox today.

LAURA goes into the ibi and returns immediately with a beer.

LAURA: (*Off.*) Lakpat?

HARSHA: Some new Icelandic NGO start up. Icelandics. They are seriously weird. One guy fell asleep, totally, like, out of it, so everyone else pissed on him. The girls as well.

LAURA: Where were you bored out of your fucking mind?

HARSHA: St. Helens.

LAURA: Pilkington glass. Rugby league.

HARSHA gulps on her beer.

HARSHA: Yeah. Wow! What fantastic beer!

LAURA: It's a German recipe. No hops. Brewed under licence in Morocco. You'll get sick of it. It's too sweet. Why Tambia?

HARSHA: I guess, I kinda just needed to do something adventurous, you know, even a bit scary. And of course, you know, I really really do want to try and make some kinda contribution, you know, on a global level. Fuck, how tossy does that sound?

LAURA: You've got an MBA.

HARSHA: So's everybody nowadays.

LAURA: On the form it said Hindu.

HARSHA: My parents are Hindu.

LAURA: Wear a veil, and tell everyone you're C of E. Sorry, would that be a problem.

HARSHA: I'm agnostic really but, like, you know, I kinda believe that God is in everything, yeah, like a kinda big organic, Gaia type thing.

LAURA: An animist?

HARSHA: Is that what I am? I do believe in a spiritual dimension. It would be weird, you know, to think that this is all there is, and you know, well, there's just so much weird stuff that can't be explained, you know er like –

LAURA: – Infinity.

HARSHA: Infinity, yeah. And poltergeists.

LAURA: Ghosts?

HARSHA: No, poltergeists. No-one disputes the existence of poltergeists, even scientists, and you know, if you accept that then you have accepted that there is another dimension.

(*Beat.*) Wow! Fuck, I went off on one, sorry.

Enter MONDAY. Dressed in western clothes, a white shirt and chinos, and leather shoes.

LAURA: This is Monday Adenuga, my husband.

They shake hands.

MONDAY: Welcome to Tambia.

HARSHA: Tambekistan

MONDAY: Very good!

HARSHA: You're the field officer, yeah?

MONDAY: That's me!

HARSHA: O.K. In Bracknell they said that men and women don't touch.

MONDAY: (*Laughing.*) Peter Nicholson.

LAURA: Have you eaten?

HARSHA: No! I'm really, like, blood sugar, zzzuuut, you know.

LAURA: We'll eat out here.

MONDAY goes off into the kitchen.

Sit down. What are we having Monday?

MONDAY: Yam foo foo.

HARSHA: Great!

LAURA: Any stew?

MONDAY: (*Off.*) I was at Enuga, in the market. I picked up some bush meat.

LAURA: Good. What is it?

MONDAY: (*Sticking his head out the window.*) Giraffe.

HARSHA: (*Hand over mouth.*) Oh no!

LAURA: It's not neck again is it?

MONDAY: You like neck.

LAURA: Be nice to have a change.

(*To HARSHA.*) Can you ride a motorbike?

HARSHA: Yes.

LAURA: What do they say about me in Bracknell?

HARSHA: Very lateral. Very creative. You make things happen.

To black.

THE END